Praise for *Play with Fire*

Everyone needs a friend like Bianca. I'm certain my mind would explode if I had two. She isn't afraid to run with knives, grab her knees and jump off big cliffs, or see how thick the ice is by running out on it. She also isn't afraid to live her life as if God's promises are really true, rather than a bunch of right-sounding doctrine we interact with by just agreeing. This isn't just a book about Bianca's journey. It's an invitation to yours. It's not a trail of bread crumbs Bianca is giving us, it's a box of matches. She dares us to light the first one, throw it back in the box we've made of our faith, and see what happens next.

–Bob Goff, *New York Times* bestselling author of *Love Does*

Bianca, thank you for being so vulnerable and sharing your story as well as the truths you've discovered along the way. This book is a treasure. If you're experiencing a struggle, desire to know God on a more passionate level, or simply want to be encouraged, you've found the perfect book!

-Kari Jobe

En fuego! Bianca is on fire. Her words form a pathway—through her own journey—to freedom and transformation. Her raw honesty and unwavering belief in God's plan for your life is contagious, and I'm excited to see how this book sparks a wildfire of faith.

–Jen Hatmaker, speaker and *New York Times* bestselling author of *For the Love*

Change and transformation isn't easy, but using her personal story and the stories of others throughout the Bible, Bianca shares with us ways to not only survive the flames of life, but THRIVE in the midst of trials. As a mentor and guide in her life, I'm excited that Bianca shares her journey to help others become the people God has called them to be through understanding the power of the Holy Spirit. Not only has Bianca written about the transforming power of God, she has lived it out.

—Christine Caine, bestselling author, teacher, and founder of A21 and Propel Women

Having the privilege of being one of Bianca's best friends since high school, I saw firsthand how she has loved, lived, and led as Jesus did. Her book, *Play with Fire*, brings a real, transparent truth with a splash of her quirky sense of humor. These are a few of the qualities that I love about her! I pray this book will ignite a fire in your life and encourage you to trust the Lord through the flames and enter into your own "Promised Land" in full faith.

—Jennie Finch, USA Olympic Softball Gold Medalist

When someone reads Bible Scriptures regarding fire, they usually interpret them within the context of sin or damnation. However, Bianca's clear voice in *Play with Fire* is carefully crafted to convey God's holy presence and the divine power to change the inner life of sincere seekers desiring a radical change. As her father and pastor, I am wholesomely proud of her work! I've witnessed my daughter transform into a woman of strength and integrity, and that is nothing short than going through a refining fire.

—Pancho Juárez, Pastor, Calvary Chapel, Montebello, California

I love this book written by my fiery Puerto Rican sister, Bianca! Her transparent stories will stir your passion and position you to flourish amid the fires of chaos, exhaustion, and confusion.

—Lisa Bevere, Messenger International, bestselling author of *Lioness Arising*, *Kissed the Girls and Made Them Cry*, and *Fight Like a Girl*

Beyond the narrative, the humorous anecdotes, and personal stories, *Play with Fire* is proof of God's redeeming love. I was reminded that fire—those painful moments in life—can refine or ruin me, but God will see to walking me through. Bianca wrote her story with grace and care as further proof that all things work together for the glory of the kingdom. Such an inspiring read!

—Jasmine Star, Branding Strategist and Marketing Consultant

Play with Fire will make you laugh, make you cry, and open your eyes to the power of God to transform your life. Bianca Juárez Olthoff has the rare ability to weave beautiful Biblical truth into her own story of transformation. You will love the power and freshness that Bianca teaches with. *Play with Fire* is the book you stay up late to finish because you can't put it down!

—Alli Worthington, author of *Breaking Busy: How to Find Peace and Purpose in a World of Crazy*

We are not defined by the fires we go through. We are defined by the fire inside of us. In *Play with Fire* Bianca Juárez Olthoff empowers women with a catalytic, Christ-centered, Bible-based infusion of passionate truth poised to awaken the *fuego* of God. Bianca does not only teach on fire, she is *on fire* for Christ, a fire that ignites her to do justice and change the world.

–Rev. Dr. Samuel Rodriguez, President of National Hispanic Christian Leadership Conference, Lead Pastor of *New Season Worship*

Bianca lives with a sincere fire for God deep in her bones. The beauty of reading her words is that same passionate fire catches in our hearts. Prepare to want more of God. Prepare to change as God's fire spreads in and through you.

–Jennie Allen, founder of IF:Gathering, author of *Restless* and *Anything*

When you play with fire, you can definitely get burned, or you might just get healed. With raw honesty, Bianca unfolds her personal journey of her time in the driest desert place. Her story of walking through the fires of life and it's purifying refinement led her to the belief that her God is not only with her, but hears her, sees and loves her dearly. She discovered, as will we, that in the desert we can have abundance and in the fire we experience the presence of God like never before.

–Shelley Giglio, Chief Strategist, sixstepsrecords and Co-founder, Passion Conferences/Passion City Church

PLAY WITH FIRE

Discovering **FIERCE FAITH**, **UNQUENCHABLE PASSION**, and a **LIFE-GIVING GOD**

BIANCA JUÁREZ OLTHOFF

ZONDERVAN

Play with Fire

Requests for information should be addressed to:
Zondervan, *3900 Sparks Dr. SE, Grand Rapids, Michigan 49546*

ISBN 978-0-310-34828-3 (audio)
ISBN 978-0-310-34525-1 (ebook)

Library of Congress Cataloging-in-Publication Data

Names: Olthoff, Bianca, author.
Title: Play with fire: discovering fierce faith, unquenchable passion, and a life-giving God / Bianca Olthoff.
Description: Grand Rapids: Zondervan, 2016.
Identifiers: LCCN 2016017736 | ISBN 9780310345244 (softcover)
Subjects: LCSH: Olthoff, Bianca. | Christian biography—United States.
Classification: LCC BR1725.O6175 A3 2016 | DDC 277.3/083092 [B]—dc23 LC record available at https://lccn.loc.gov/2016017736

The author is represented by Alive Literary Agency, 7680 Goddard Street, Suite 200, Colorado Springs, Colorado 80920, www.aliveliterary.com.

Cover design: Darren Welsh Design
Cover photo: Roxana Gonzalez / Shutterstock®
Interior design: Kait Lamphere

First printing June 2016 / Printed in the United States of America

To you, my dear friend—
May you remember those dreams you once had
That you held on to dearly
May you resurrect them and boldly step into the fire
That will transform you so clearly

Contents

The Legend of the Phoenix

The caterpillar into the butterfly. The duckling into the swan. The peasant into the princess. Since childhood I've been obsessed with the idea of transformation. Perhaps it was because I wanted to shed my skin and emerge as something different the way children do. Still, at the core of my soul, I have always believed change is possible.

In college I read the rising of the phoenix as part of a project on Greek mythology, and a spark ignited within me like a match to tinder. Something about the story of this bird—going into the desert, crying out to a silent sun, rising from ashes to fly home—moved my soul and gave me hope. The legend has been told and retold over years and cultures. This tale's oral tradition can be traced back to Greek, Egyptian, Japanese, Chinese, and Persian cultures. But to early church fathers like Clement and Lactantius, the phoenix was a symbol of resurrection, rebirth, and renewal. As I read the story, however, the phoenix was more than a faraway fable or symbol of faith. It was me.

My life was in flames, and I had nowhere to turn.

I don't know if it was the bird's loneliness or the isolation or the hiding or the silence or the desire to be transformed that resonated with me the most, but I lost myself in the prose of ancient times. The myth seemed to give me a bird's-eye view of my own story. As I read about the exhausted bird traveling in desperation to an isolated desert, I caught a glimpse of my own life and the promise that one day I—like the phoenix—would be made new.

The myth awakened in me a reality many of us face. There will be proverbial fires that threaten our lives, moments that make us feel like all hope is gone and nothing can or will ever change. But I want to remind you, the fire that can be dangerous is the same fire that can refine and transform. It's not about our circumstances; it's about what we're made of.

In the loneliest of times, we have a wondrous opportunity to discover a deity who is not far away, but close; not silent, but speaking; not incapable, but incredible. It is *that* God who took me through the fire like Shadrach, Meshach, and Abednego to reveal His presence.

I'm sharing these stories with you, dear friend, because I believe we can be transformed in the midst of chaos, exhaustion, and confusion. In the deepest fiber of my being, I believe that when we go through life's fires, we will rise transformed. No, our transformation won't be the result of mythical fire from a silent sun as it was for the phoenix, but we will go through the fire like Shadrach, Meshach, and Abednego. We will experience the presence of the one true God, the creator of fire. Unlike the mythical gods of ancient times, our bold requests for transformation will be heard by God, who will resurrect us to new life through the power of His Son, Jesus Christ.

Rise from the ashes . . .

Part ONE

Chapter **ONE**

The Crisis

This was my quarter-life crisis. It was 2003, and I was sitting on my parents' couch, bags of carbohydrates all around, eating my sorrows away while I zoned out on midday television. I was a college graduate. I'd received my diploma with promise and pomp, only to meet the workforce with rejection and deflation. A single woman (by circumstance, not choice), I felt ghastly and unwanted. I lived with my parents, ate their food, and watched television on their couch. I was in the middle of an incinerator, flames all around me, and I watched as all my promise turned to ash.

What does a college graduate do when she is jobless and can't even find an internship when she's willing to work for free? Well, if it's me, she binges on chips, stuffs her face with sugary carbs, and watches *Oprah*, of course.

As I watched, Oprah welcomed Jacqui Saburido, and when the young woman entered the camera's frame, I was taken aback. Her marred skin was cinched and taut, paper thin and nearly transparent. Pockmarked and knobbed, her shoulders jutted out sharply, highlighting her disfigured face. After introductions, the screen displayed a photograph of a beautiful

Hispanic girl with long black hair and an inviting smile as Oprah shared Jacqui's story. She grew up in Venezuela, studied engineering in college, and dreamed of taking over her father's manufacturing business, getting married, and having children.

In 1999, Jacqui moved to the United States to study English in Austin, Texas. One month later, tragedy struck. As she was driving home with friends one night, a drunk driver collided with her car. Jacqui's legs were pinned under the dashboard, and her vehicle erupted in flames. As a paramedic who was on the scene described it, "When Jacqui was engulfed by the flames, she was screaming and moaning and wailing an almost inhuman sound that I'd never heard another person make."

Jacqui's skin burned for nearly a minute before the paramedics could free her from the car. She was beyond recognition—her skin, her hair, and her face had melted away. She lay in a hospital, unconscious, for ten months. Jacqui's life, once independent, now revolved around hospitals, doctors, and the numerous surgeries needed to rebuild her face and body.

When Oprah interviewed her four years later, Jacqui spoke of her dreams, said she was still whole and beautiful in her mind's eye. "I feel . . . of course, not physically, but inside . . . I feel like the same person." This small woman with deep, sunken eyes and bird-like frailty possessed a palpable strength. Her inner beauty emanated beyond her outward appearance and her inner strength belied her fragile-looking physique. She only allowed herself to cry for five minutes a day and said she was glad she survived the accident.

Jacqui cried only five minutes a day, but I wept through the entire show. I stared at this woman with her disfigured hands, grafted body, and scarred face, and I nodded as Oprah referred to her as the personification of inner beauty and strength.

Jacqui rose from the ashes a survivor.

Listening to the brave woman who emerged from fire ignited something in me. It stirred my passion and made me want to forego living with caution. With the dramatic optimism and zeal that characterizes twentysomethings, I wanted to throw down my bag of chips, get off the couch, and do something important. I wanted my life to be consumed by the fire of transformation.

Chapter **TWO**

God, Are You There?

I am the reflection of my people, those émigrés who believed in the intrinsic right to life, liberty, and the pursuit of happiness. My mother's family moved to the United States from Puerto Rico. An immigrant herself, my mother fell in love with an immigrant from Mexico, and they committed to creating a life in the concrete jungles of East Los Angeles.

My father supported our family by working multiple jobs. Whether it was laying tile, cutting down trees, or working as a cook in the cafeteria of Azusa Pacific University, he did everything he could to provide. But feeding a family of six on a single income—especially one as meager as my father's—was hard, and we often needed a straight-up miracle to make ends meet, a Jesus-feeding-the-masses-with-five-loaves-and-two-fishes type of miracle.

The call to ministry runs deep in our family, and when my father planted a church in Los Angeles, the whole family pitched in. His dream became our dream, and we committed to loving people in our community. Most people avoid the ghetto, but my parents desired to create an oasis of hope amid the streets of East L.A. It was difficult and burdensome, but my parents served the church well. I watched them juggle the responsibilities of leading people, providing for their family, teaching God's Word, and raising their children (and all the other crazy kids who attended the church).

In those early years of church planting, God provided in amazing ways. We didn't own a house, we didn't even have a car, but we were in the presence and fullness of God, and knew that what we had was far greater than three gourmet meals a day in a mansion with a Bentley in the garage but without God.

Amidst the tension of want and need, we knew God would provide. Life was beautiful, but difficult; beautifully difficult, I suppose you could say. I was often mocked and marginalized for my lack of stylish clothes. (We were po'. So poor we couldn't afford a second *O*, much less the *R*. Yes, just po'.) I remember being in Sunday school seeing all the cool kids were decked out in their L.A. Gear shoes and trendy clothes. (Let's pause for a moment of solidarity over how cool L.A. Gear was and mourn the fact that triple-laced shoes no longer exist.) I dreamed of being popular and cool enough to sit with the L.A. Gear crew. I begged my mom for a pair of the stylish sneakers, but I was told time and time again we could not afford them.

I kept hope alive for those shoes, and one magical day at Pic 'n Save, a discount clearance store, I spotted a pair of white, studded, triple-laced Michael Jackson L.A. Gear shoes on an otherwise empty shelf. These shoes were the living dream of what I imagined cool people wore, and they were *my size*. It was as though the celestials opened and Michael the archangel moonwalked down from heaven to place the coolest shoes on the clearance rack just for me.

I ran to my mother and told her I would never ask for

anything else as long as I lived if she bought the shoes for me. Holding my breath, I silently prayed she would say the shoes were within our budget. That day, I walked out of Pic 'n Save carrying a white plastic bag and feeling as rich as Michael Jackson himself.

On Sunday, I wore my brand-new shoes and walked over to where all the cool kids hung out. I thought they would accept me, that I'd have the opportunity to hang out with them because I finally had what they had. But the seats weren't open for me, and the girls said I couldn't sit with them. I was devastated. I walked in my white, studded, triple-laced Michael Jackson L.A. Gear shoes to an empty table and sat alone, confronted by my greatest fear: *I would never have what I needed to be who I wanted to be.*

We knew poverty; we knew the sting of not being socially accepted. But God always seemed to provide. One particular day, when the fridge was empty and the pantry bare, my mother pulled out a large piece of butcher paper and taped it to the kitchen door. On the top of the page, she wrote PRAYER LIST in thick, bold letters. With earnest humility and brazen faith, she told us that we serve a God who hears our prayers and answers them in His perfect time.

She gave us each a marker and told us to list what we needed.

- Grandpa's salvation
- A car
- Food
- A building for church
- Outfits for Easter (This was mine. Obviously.)

As the list grew, we poured out prayers for each need. We bowed our heads, closed our eyes, and asked God to provide for us just as He provided for the children of Israel. We knew God provided water, manna, quail, and daily provisions while the Israelites were in the desert. Why couldn't He do the same for us?

That very afternoon, one of our neighbors stumbled onto our front porch with a heavy box of bread, government-issued cheese, yogurt, and butter. My mother graciously received the box of food and thanked our neighbor profusely. As she shut the front door, the heavy box slipped from her weary arms. She pulled us around the dining room table. Pointing to the prayer list, she said, "The Lord has heard our prayers! See? He's already answered us." Her belief unwavering, she instilled in us the kind of faith gained through experience, won through battle, and revealed through perseverance.

We watched as our mother slathered butter on slices of bread and placed them in a sizzling hot pan. She cut pieces of cheese from the five-pound block, and placed them atop the grilled bread. The butter bubbled and filled the kitchen with an aroma so delicious, I'm almost positive Jesus Himself would have salivated over her culinary masterpiece. (Note: If you've never had a grilled cheese sandwich made with government-issued cheese, you've **never** had a grilled cheese sandwich!) She took the sandwiches from the pan and put them on our plates. The cheese oozed from the corners of the bread's crispy edges as my mother cut our sandwiches into triangles. Then, holding hands, we sat around our dining room table, across from our prayer list, and thanked God for hearing us in our time of need.

The prayer list (which was eventually answered in full),

the faith of my mother, the grilled cheese sandwiches, the kind neighbor, the marked moment of gratitude around our table, it all came together perfectly like the butter, bread, and cheese to form something delicious. Psalm 34:8 says, "Taste and see that the Lord is good." And let me tell you, His provision tasted even better than those buttery sandwiches!

Whether through donated food boxes or hand-me-down clothes from people at church, or anonymous cashier's checks mailed to our house, our needs were always met by a God who heard our cries. I watched as God provided for us in undoubtedly supernatural ways. But still, my young mind missed the message in these miracles: God provides what we need when we need it.

BINGE

Even as God provided for my family, I lacked faith that He would provide for me in other ways. I found solace in stealing food and bingeing in secret. Carbs, sugar, and fat were my three amigos. They made me feel safe. I binged in pantries, hid under my bed with crackers, and sneaked loaves of bread into the garage. I enjoyed these private indulgences.

As amazing as my mother's grilled cheeses were, and as providential as gifted yogurts may have been, I began to seek comfort in food. No longer was God sustaining me and giving me joy; instead, food was. When boys on the playground made fun of my cankles, waistline, and uniboob, I pretended to be unfazed by their caustic words but later drowned my embarrassment in a secret gallon of ice cream or bag of chips.

Sean Korriega, who found particular joy in making fun of me, was the leader of the Bianca-bashing crew at church. I remember playing kickball after Sunday school and kicking a home run over Sean, who was the pitcher. As I happily ran the bases, I saw Sean and the boys wobbling around as if on unsure footing. He yelled out as I rounded third base, "Whoooooooa! Every time you run, it feels like an earthquake! Run for your life before Bianca causes tectonic shifts in California!" I ran to home base and said I had to go to the bathroom, but I hid in the supply cabinet, eating animal cookies out of the clear tub reserved for the preschoolers' snack time.

The mockery didn't end with my cellulite or saddlebags. When I was eleven, my classmates mocked my inability to read. When I stuttered or struggled to sound out words, I excused it, saying I needed my glasses and couldn't read without them. Inevitably, I found myself sneaking into the pantry with a spoon and diving into a container of crunchy peanut butter.

Although I witnessed the faithfulness of God to meet my basic needs, I used coping mechanisms to meet my immediate, personal needs. I frequently forgot the ways God answered my prayers, and I began looking elsewhere for comfort. Food was my way of anesthetizing my emotions and numbing my embarrassment. It was my socially acceptable drug.

Before I could spell the word *obese*, I weighed more than my father. At the age of eleven, I stood four feet ten inches tall and weighed one hundred and eighty pounds; I wasn't *chubby* or *fluffy* anymore; I was simply obese. One area of our family's divine provision—food—became my prison, and I cried out to God in sheer desperation.

I can't tell you what spawned my emotional tailspin on one

particular day, but I can tell you what I was eating. The grass prickled my back as I lay on the ground, looking up at the sky with a glass plate, warm to the touch, balanced on my belly. The conversations I had with God as an eleven-year-old are embarrassingly similar to the conversations I still have with God as an adult. *Do You see me? Will You answer my prayers? Can You please change this?*

I found myself crying out to God, *I can't live like this.* With the warm plate teetering on my belly, I picked up a gloopy piece of ghetto fondue and plopped it into my mouth. (Recipe: [1] Cut a block of cheese into chunks. [2] Place the cheese on a plate in the microwave. [3] Nuke it for thirty seconds. Voila! Ghetto fondue.) I didn't like the person I was, but I didn't know how to change. I begged God to show up, be strong, answer my prayers, and transform me from the stupid, fat, poor, brown girl living on Meeker Street, into a girl who believed there was a plan and a purpose for her life, a way to live in the fullness of His faithfulness, a way to be a leader and not the last one picked for the kickball team.

God, can You hear me? Are You there? I didn't want to be the person I was, but I didn't know how to change.

Chapter **THREE**

Chosen

Sunday school was my safe haven, replete with small desks, plastic chairs, and Precious Moments Bibles. It was my place to be with a God who was for me. Every Sunday I ran my hand along the walls of the church corridors as I made my way into the fifth-grade classroom to help Mr. Charles wipe down the chalkboards and set up the chairs before class.

Mr. Charles was my favorite Sunday school teacher. With his weathered hands, dark chocolate skin, and deep voice, he painted a picture of God that was mesmerizing. As a guide leading us on a journey, his melodic baritone and slight Southern drawl—as sweet as a hint of honey—took us on an adventure every week. He wasn't overly animated or showy like most Sunday school teachers, but he was like Moses, who led his people to freedom.

Each week Mr. Charles wrote prayer requests on the chalkboard. Each week I asked him to add my prayer request—I wanted to visit Israel. At first the other students, and even Mr. Charles himself, thought it was weird that a kid asked to leave the country on some sort of adolescent pilgrimage. But each week my request remained the same, and each week he pressed the white chalk on the green board, scratching in his distinct writing, *Bianca to go the Holy Land, Israel.* It was so predictable that eventually, when I raised my hand, he nodded at me and turned around to write my prayer request even before I finished speaking. He knew what I was going to ask before I asked it, and he always encouraged me to ask God for what I needed and wanted.

Mr. Charles taught from the Old Testament Scriptures about a chosen people group—the Israelites, God's chosen people—who were called out of oppression and promised a land of abundance. Moving from slavery to success, from poverty to prosperity, God's chosen children were given what was promised to them: freedom and land. Mr. Charles, an African American man with a Southern heritage, spoke with the fervency of his own reality. He spoke of God's freedom, and he smiled as if freedom were a cold glass of sweet tea on a scorching, humid day.

"Mmm hmm, it's true," he said. "As God's chosen children, you too can cry out to God to rescue you, and He will save you. There is *nothing* our great God can't do." The word *nothing* was weighted with such emphasis I couldn't help but believe him. For the first time in my young life, I understood what being chosen meant. It meant God wanted you and wanted to use you. But had I ever felt chosen? I was always picked last for kickball, never in first place, and didn't fit in. I knew love from my parents, but nothing of being chosen.

The way Mr. Charles spoke about the Israelites, their Promised Land, and what they overcame to get there resonated deep in my chest, ached in my bones. I didn't want to be a slave to food, to my own self-criticism or the unending, heartless taunts of the cool kids. I wanted to be free. I wanted to get to the place where the chosen resided. I wanted the Holy Land, Israel. Maybe, just *maybe*, if I got there, I would be chosen too.

FOR ME

When you're the product of a low-income area, words of affirmation and hope from adults can be as rare as graffiti-free walls. Having a plan and purpose in life felt as foreign as having a pool in the backyard or going on a European vacation. But I held on to the words of Mr. Charles and the faith of my mother and started to believe that the promises in the Bible weren't just for pretty, polished, perfect people. They were for me too.

Every night my father prayed blessings over his growing family while he tucked us into bed. As he kissed our foreheads and turned off the bedroom lights, he told us we were beautiful and loved. My twin sister had external headgear that protruded from her mouth, I had thick tortoiseshell glasses, and as I mentioned earlier, we both weighed more than he did (don't judge; our freckles were heavy!). Although I felt neither beautiful nor lovable, I believed my father in the same way I believed Mr. Charles. I knew God loved me and had a plan for me. Just as I believed my biological father, I knew I had to trust my heavenly Father.

Longing to be chosen and confident in God's love, I began choosing to appropriate the promises of God as my own. If God was for me, I *must* have been chosen. If His Word was for me, so were all the promises it held in its pages. Despite the taunts, jeers, and shaming words of church kids and neighborhood kids alike, I developed a new sense of faith. My life and circumstances didn't change. My family lived in a small house with no air conditioning next door to a schizophrenic neighbor who grew and sold marijuana in his backyard. We shopped at thrift stores and bargain bins. Crack addicts looking for a cheap hit broke into our house and robbed us. But in the midst of this, as my faith grew, I began to *believe* I was chosen. And I knew I was promised a life that looked different from the one I was living.

In a wide-ruled spiral-bound notebook, I wrote down Bible verses as if they were written especially for me. Jesus told me, "You did not choose me, but *I chose you* and appointed you that you might go and bear fruit—fruit that will last—and so that whatever you ask in my name the Father will give you" (John 15:16, emphasis mine).

Maybe it was desperation. Maybe it was childlike foolishness. Maybe it was real faith. Whatever the motivation, my eleven-year-old self began to believe God was *for* me and *chose* me. God wanted me to be on His kickball team at recess and by His side and to hold on to His promises. I believed it.

CHOSEN

The children of Israel held on to the promises of God even when things didn't make sense—that was the way Mr. Charles put it. Under the thumb of the pharaoh, Egypt's worshiped ruler, the Israelites endured over four hundred years of slavery.

They worked nonstop, and were mistreated and undervalued. But as Mr. Charles taught us, the book of Deuteronomy shows that the Israelites were chosen by God to be His chosen people. Being chosen, then, clearly doesn't mean being comfortable.

The oppression the Israelites experienced, the abuse they endured, and the abandonment they must have felt seeped deep into their hearts. But here's what I know—the chosen people of God cried out to God for rescue. They asked for what they needed.

BEING CHOSEN, THEN, CLEARLY DOESN'T MEAN BEING COMFORTABLE.

It's easy to say this now—isn't hindsight always more clear?—but when I cried out to God, He listened. He responded. In the darkest moments of my childhood depression, God heard my cries. And even now, when life is as dry and barren as the desert of Sinai, God knows my pain. The Scriptures put it this way: "The Israelites groaned in their slavery and cried out, and their cry for help because of their slavery went up to God . . . The LORD said, 'I have indeed seen the misery of my people in Egypt. I have heard them crying out because of their slave drivers, and I am concerned about their suffering'" (Ex. 2:23; 3:7).

A GREAT GOD

As I lay in the warm grass with my plate of ghetto fondue balanced on my belly, I thought of the Israelites and this promise. Although I didn't experience crazy shaking or celestial light from heaven, I felt something inside, just like I did when Mr.

Charles spoke of freedom; it was deep in my chest and ached in my bones. I remembered our tattered butcher paper prayer list and how God had been faithful to miraculously provide. I knew then that I needed not only to believe, but had to *behave* as though the Scriptures weren't just for rich people who were skinny and could spell. I had to turn my faith into action the way my mother had shown me. Maybe the rich promises of hope, redemption, and reparation in the Bible *were* for me. I was God's *chosen*. In a world where I felt marginalized, overlooked, and ignored, He chose me.

In that moment, I prayed a big prayer—the biggest prayer my eleven-year-old self could pray. I promised God that if He would give me words, I would give Him my voice. I had no idea what that really meant, but it sounded good. It was what I was moved to pray. I confessed that I didn't want to be the stupid kid anymore, and I simply and honestly believed God could help me.

Over the following months, my mother was shocked to see a sudden shift in my comprehension and reading retention. Don't get me wrong; I was no genius or anything, but my reading skills grew rapidly. I stayed up reading in bed with a flashlight, took books along when my mother and I ran errands, and chose reading at home over playing with the neighborhood kids (this did nothing for my thickening waistline). Once I knew I could read, I felt empowered. A new world opened up, and I discovered that what I could read, I could learn. Knowledge became power, and I obsessively inhaled books like they were fresh loaves of bread. I was going to change my life. I wasn't going to be the stupid dumb kid anymore.

Although my mother took our education seriously, formal methods of schooling weren't her priority. A hippie at heart, my mom was in a homeschool co-op (yes, I said *co-op*; didn't I mention she was a hippie?). She subscribed to the tenets of Dr. Raymond Moore's *Better Late than Early,* and wasn't worried about state-mandated testing as she taught us with backyard art projects and hands-on science experiments. The first time we took state standardized tests, my sister and I earned embarrassingly low scores, yet I'm not sure my mom was worried that her eleven-year-old twins couldn't read.

When the time came for California state aptitude testing a few months later, I sat nervously at a small desk in a cavernous room with forty other homeschooled children. On my desk were a booklet, a Scantron test form, and three well-sharpened pencils. I stared at the other kids in the room and tried not to think about how they looked smarter than me. I anxiously tapped my pencil on the desk and prayed a quick prayer. Mr. Charles had assured me God *would be* faithful. My mother had shown me He *would be* faithful. God Himself promised that He always *would be* faithful. I desperately trusted Him with my learning, and with this test. With my eyes squeezed shut as the teacher said, "Begin, class," I asked God to help me, and I plunged into the test.

The test results arrived in the mail weeks later, and we waited until my father came home from work to open the envelopes containing our scores. I anxiously tore mine open and read the results out loud to my parents. Confused, my mother asked in near disbelief to see what was written on the paper I held. Not only had I achieved significant increases on the comprehension and retention components of the test, but I had demonstrated the reading level of an eleventh-grade student. With pride and joy, my mother handed the test results back to me. I felt like I was holding a letter from God Himself. In my hand was a tangible sign that God had heard my prayer. Just as He heard the cries of the Israelites during their time of oppression in Egypt, He heard the cry of a little girl with big dreams.

I twirled barefoot in the kitchen and threw my arms around the waist of my beaming mother. "I prayed God would help me read, and He did!" I cried. I heard the words of Mr. Charles ringing in my head: "Mmm hmm, it's true. There is *nothing* our great God can't do."

The song of my heart had been deep and earnest. In the midst of my pain and frustration, there was hope. *I was chosen.* "If You give me words," I had promised, "I will give You my voice." There on the cool linoleum floor, I danced in celebration of God's faithfulness and at the top of my lungs, I praised Him.

Chapter **FOUR**

Reinvention

I decided to treat the year I started college as a time for reinvention. For me, this meant shedding both weight and shame. While things had significantly improved for me academically, I still struggled with weight, worth, and an exhausting desire to fit in. Leaving home was my chance, I thought, and I worked tirelessly to sever all connection to my childhood life. I ritually reminded myself that no one on campus knew I was once an illiterate child who shared a bedroom with my twin sister and snuck food into closets when no one was looking. No one I met knew I was poor or made fun of me because of where I lived or the color of my skin. No one in my dorm knew I'd witnessed prejudice against my father and his lingering accent. I buried the shadow of the little girl who hid under blankets in the recesses of my mind. I ignored the memory of my first reinvention, my God-given metamorphosis at the tender age of eleven, and went on to pursue my own selfish attempt at transformation.

I was determined to appear utterly flawless. From color-coding and rewriting my notes to attending study groups and creating note cards, I was obsessed with my academic performance. I would have done almost anything to earn an A. And my maniacal behavior didn't stop there. I became obsessed with dieting and achieving an elusive number on the scale. I fixated on controlling every aspect of my life, and believed it was up to me to ensure I would never be made fun of again. *I* had the power to guarantee I'd be chosen first for the college equivalent of a kickball game, and *I* could diet (read: starve) myself into clothing that was hip and trendy instead of having to shop in the plus-size section of a department store. Never again would I need to wear an extra large forest green jumpsuit with elastic waistband and faux gold buttons (AKA my Easter outfit, circa 1989).

I can't even begin to recall how many diets I've been on, but seriously, it's an embarrassing number. The Orange Peel Diet (boil thirty orange rinds for five hours in two gallons of water and drink the tea for the next forty-eight hours). The Soup Diet (boil every green vegetable in a cauldron of water and eat it for eight days straight). The Meat Diet (the diabolic travesty of my life, for which my intestines have yet to forgive me). The Vegan Diet (I gained weight). The Liquid Diet (I ran to the restroom every thirty seconds). The Pills-from-Mexico Diet (I not only lost weight; I lost sleep, hair, and control over my sweat glands). Sadly, I could go on.

I tried to control every situation in my life with micro-managed precision. I lost forty-five pounds, I earned a stellar GPA, and I dressed only in the trendiest clothes. My work was excellent, my professors loved me, and my scholarships kept coming in. I, I, I. My, my, my. Me, me, me. I was the captain of my ship, the driver of the vehicle I called destiny, the god of my own life.

I was certain that other people thought I had my life together, and if I'm being honest, I'll have to admit that was what I wanted. But my heart knew it was a ruse. The accolades, accomplishments, and affirmation did nothing for my soul. My achievements never satisfied me, never made me feel like I was enough, like I had purpose, or like I mattered.

Deep inside, I was paralyzed by the fear that one misstep would cause a trapdoor to open and a massive boulder to fall on my head. One mistake would cancel out the favor in my life and reveal the frightened girl beneath who appeared to control everything but actually controlled nothing. I was placing all importance on the provision, not the Provider.

I see it now. In spite of how much I loved God, I'd fully managed to quit trusting Him. I knew He had promised a land flowing with milk and honey for the Israelites, just like Mr. Charles said, and somewhere inside I believed He could provide that land for me. But He just wasn't moving fast enough, and I was trying to take that land by force.

The answered prayers and fulfilled promises of God—those in Scripture and in my own experience—all pointed to a God who could bring breakthroughs and answers. But I wanted them on my terms. My inner control freak whispered game plans and quick fixes for everything from minor daily concerns to the broader strategies for achieving my long-term goals. And every single thing she uttered sounded better to me than trusting the Lord and waiting patiently.

When exams stressed me out, my mother always quoted Isaiah 40:31 ("But those who trust in the LORD will find new strength. They will soar high on wings like eagles. They will run and not grow weary. They will walk and not faint"—NLT).

"But," I'd respond with an eye roll, in an exasperated tone, "who has time for that?!"

I invited God on the journey *I* mapped out, rather than waiting for Him to tell me where to go. Waistlines had to be slimmed down, plans had to be made, life had to be orchestrated. God would catch up when He could, but I wasn't going to wait for Him.

It's both a cosmic and a spiritual rule: although taking control sounds good in theory, the actual outworking eventually fails. As the Yiddish adage states, "If you want to make God laugh, tell Him your plans." What the saying fails to include is this: "If you tell God your plans, He might just disrupt them and send you into the desert."

THE DESERT

The proverbial desert is a lonely, isolated place. Many people are dropped into its infertile expanse by way of an unexpected crisis or an unforeseen loss.

This is your two-week notice.

Your father and I are getting divorced.

You weren't accepted.

You have cancer.

I'm pregnant.

We lost the house.

I don't love you anymore.

With only a few words, a terse phrase, we can find ourselves ripped from our comfort zones and wandering in the desert. We tumble from stability into unemployment. We are hurled from a relationship into the land of singleness. We wither in the valley of grief. We learn new medical language, become acquainted with the stages of cancer, live with treatments more debilitating than the disease itself.

But for each one of us transported to the desert by way of life's circumstances, others find it by way of our own willfulness. We try to control every outcome. We strive to achieve and accomplish. We become self-sufficient, and in so doing, we walk away from the God who wants to lead us into His provision, onto His green pathways.

Whether circumstance or our own willfulness brings us into the desert, one truth remains constant: the terrain is unknown and frightening. We may have grown up hearing sermons out of Romans about how all things work for good for those who love God, but in the desert? In the desert every vision of provision is a mirage, and we find ourselves at a loss as to how to navigate the landscape.

We all go through desert seasons and have the opportunity to determine how we will respond. The cyclical frustrations I faced in regard to my desire for control, fear, and the longing to feel chosen were the catalysts that initiated my time in the desert. I longed to create my own transformation. I wanted to be chosen. I wanted to be in control, and following my own way, I found myself in a dry and weary place. And I couldn't navigate my way out.

What is Control? She is a woman with fabulous hair and defined biceps. She is the straight-A student, the high-achieving executive. She is always two steps ahead. Her favorite word is yes, and she can deliver results to anyone.

And although Control is impossible to pin down, I chased

her. I wanted to be her. I thought I *could* be her. I followed Control's lead—hair, biceps, straight As and all. I said yes to everyone. *Yes* made me feel like I was in control of the outcome, and that the results depended on me alone. *Yes* gave me the illusion that I could deliver joy and happiness to others, as well as to myself. *If you take this demanding job, you will have the financial freedom you always wanted.* Yes, I'll take it. *If you copy this essay, you will be guaranteed an A.* Yes, I will do it. *If you try this diet pill, it will make you lose twenty-four pounds in twenty-four hours.* Yes, I'll pop that pill.

But Control is a manipulator. She promises what can't be had. She promises perfection.

While I chased after Control and envied her apparent freedom, God called after me, tried to remind me that Control was my own construct. I know this now. Looking back, I can see that no matter how perfect my wardrobe was, how thin my waist became, or how much education I obtained, nothing made me feel secure. Ironically, I couldn't *control* myself out of my own desert. The more I tried, the drier, hotter, and more desolate it became. God watched as I proved that my plan to micromanage every second of my life only led me deeper into desolation. He knew the futility of my attempts, and like a patient father, He waited for me to understand that I needed to entrust my life to Him.

THE ROOT OF IT ALL

I'm more of an aboveground type of girl, as in, I like the stuff you can see. Flowers, trees, and vegetation symbolize life, growth, and transformation. The problem with focusing on external manifestations, though, is we don't see what is beneath the topsoil. If a root structure is shallow, nothing will stand. And when the topsoil is stripped dry? There's very little in the way of tangible life.

To survive and even thrive in the desert, plants must send their roots deep to push into hidden springs to find life-giving water. Humans are no different. In the desert seasons of life, we must root into the goodness of God, into being known and loved by God. We need to be rooted in our identities as the beloved creations of a merciful and divine Creator. We store these truths, allow them to spur growth, to deepen our roots, to bring us to bloom in even the most trying terrain.

During my college years, I was exhausted and depleted from trying to build my perfect American Dream life. The things I once loved and believed promised me freedom—weight loss, money, and perfection—were only shallow roots. I spent so much time on the external that the internal was malnourished and withering. Instead of believing I had value and worth because I was loved by God, I believed my worth came from being loved by others, and I focused my efforts there. I wanted to bloom with popularity and perfection, not to endure the pruning that leads to maturity. I assumed being in control would guarantee a life of ease, and when it proved to be the opposite, I found myself rotting in the desert I had created through my need for that control.

I wish I had considered the story of the Israelites in Exodus 16. God's chosen people were wandering in their own desert, spiritually in need and still complaining about what they lacked. They'd ignored the instructions of the Lord to boldly enter into the Promised Land, following their own directions instead. As a result, they wandered in the desert wilderness. They wanted freedom and the Promised Land, but their actions showed a lack of trust in the promises of God. They failed to root themselves in the promises of God, and so their metaphorical roots were beginning to shrivel. They became exhausted, discouraged, and doubtful of God's goodness, and began to starve, both physically and spiritually. In fact, they grumbled against Moses and Aaron saying, "If only we had died by the Lord's hand in Egypt! There we sat around pots of meat and ate all the food we wanted, but you have brought us out into this desert to starve this entire assembly to death" (Ex. 16:3).

That's melodramatic, even for a Latina!

The truth is, I was no different. I wanted to lead myself out of the desert, tried to get out by way of perfectionism. I hustled; *doing* was more important than *being*. I knew the church game and felt like I did all the right things: I served at church, tithed regularly, kept a journal, and read *The One Year Bible*. But it was hard for me to believe my spiritual works were enough, and when I failed, I believed, like the Israelites, that I was going to die without having what I thought I needed. In those moments, I'd grumble against God with my own "WHY DO YOU HATE ME?!" tantrums. When I did poorly on a project or missed the mark on a task, I fell apart. It's been said if you live by applause, you'll die by criticism. I defined my success—even my worth—by the judgments and opinions of others. When those opinions were less than I'd hoped for, I was utterly destroyed. I was disconnected from the true source of life in those desert days, and I was dying, withering in the desert.

DOUBTING THE GOODNESS OF GOD IN THE DESERT

The desert is a lonely place, and it's easy to feel forgotten, unseen, or abandoned. In my desert, I no longer saw (or allowed myself to see) the goodness of God because I had decided it wasn't enough. When I didn't get what I wanted or things didn't run on my timetable, I felt like everyone else was getting the things I deserved. In those dry, desert moments, it's easy to feel alone. But as Deuteronomy 31:8 promises, "The Lord himself goes before you and will be with you; he will never leave you nor forsake you. Do not be afraid; do not be discouraged."

Growing up poor inevitably poses the danger that you will live the rest of your life with a scarcity mentality, a chronic fear of not having enough and holding too tightly to what you do have. During an economic recession, my father faced a desert season while he fought daily to find a job. But every day, whether or not he had an income, we had enough food for our family.

And here, during my college years, those fears caught up with me. Instead of evolving and maturing in my relationship with God, I mixed my faith with a dose of elbow grease and control, hoping I might have some say in the outcome. The fact that I had a decorative pillow on my dorm room bed with Psalm 46:10 embroidered on it didn't mean I was ever "still" enough to "know [He was] God." I was holding on to the old because I was afraid God wouldn't provide the new.

Amidst all the noise of my own thrashing, I didn't hear the still, small voice of God. He was whispering, "I'm here. Stop running. I will lead you out of this desert season," but I was deaf to His promise of provision.

Part

TWO

Chapter **FIVE**

Breaking

I was nearing my twenty-first birthday, and what should have been a time of celebration and excitement was shrouded with pressure and performance. I wore my perfectionism like a two-ton party hat.

My mother had not been feeling well for several months, and met with doctors and specialists to try to diagnose her illness. While she was shuffled to and from appointments and checked in and out of the hospital, my twin sister and I shared the responsibility of taking care of our youngest siblings. Cooking, cleaning, teaching, reprimanding, and all things surrogate mother related were piled atop my packed schedule as a full-time student and part-time swim coach.

My days started with workouts before the sun rose, as I tried to keep my weight in check. Then I studied and completed homework assignments before transitioning to a full day of classes. I was on an academic scholarship and studied around the clock to maintain a perfect grade point average. Furiously racing to classes, to work, to study groups, and to workshops, I fought to maintain the illusion of perfection and the promise of fulfillment (meaning: one day I would be so happy with my life, I would want nothing else). The struggle to balance the demands of life and academic expectations was almost more than I could bear.

After class, I made my way to the pool, where I coached my swim team well into the evening. All my remaining time was spent with my ailing mother and family. Whether it was tutoring my siblings, cleaning the house, or just spending time with my mom, I felt the pressure of all my striving.

As if the workload were not enough, my desire to be desired was overwhelming. I was in a long-term dysfunctional relationship. He was older and smarter and wiser and cooler and all the things I wasn't. He was tattooed, pierced, and the lead singer in a growing band. I couldn't believe he wanted me. That was the problem. I think we were both confused about why he dated me, a straight-laced college girl who actually believed in the use of shampoo.

After every breakup (yes, we broke up multiple times), I went into a tailspin, believing it was the width of my thighs or the style of my clothing that caused him to leave. We swung like a pendulum—deeply in love or deeply in pain—but we always seemed to find a way back to each other. I looked to him for affirmation; he looked to me for stability. I felt chosen, the very thing I longed for, by someone who seemed to be desired by everyone else. He felt stable because I was tethered to the place he called home. We both lost focus on what really mattered, and our complicated relationship hit a high—or maybe I should say a low—point around my twenty-first birthday. The man I loved broke my heart into what felt like a million grains of sand, and scattered them on what was already sinking land.

My life was imploding as he traveled around the United States in the band, calling me from new hotel rooms in different cities, living a life far removed from my pain. I wanted him near, but he came only so close. I told him how I felt, expressed my frustration, shared my pain and begged him to act like a boyfriend should. His apologies and promises were uttered in such melodic tones, you would have thought he was singing. I was wooed time and time again, lulled into being the passive girl I never believed I could be.

One day, when he was on tour and in a new hotel room in a distant city, he called to tell me it was over. I had too much potential, and I was too good for him. Or at least, that's what he told me. I didn't feel like I had potential. I didn't feel too good for him.

My life was held together by a thread, but I still fought for the illusion of perfection and tried to maintain control. I was heartbroken and needed someone to comfort me. My mother, usually a great source of comfort, was growing more and more ill, and was unable to care for me. She was in her own medical tailspin, and the doctors still didn't know why. And so, without anyone to give me comfort, and without the proper time to grieve, I bottled up my emotions and turned my focus to my mother.

Stepping into adulthood was supposed to make me feel grown up and ready to start my life. Instead, I felt lost and confused. I was mothering my mother, taking care of kids who were not my own, fighting to keep up appearances, and desperately trying to lose another ten pounds. Yes, I was in the desert, but I clung to the belief that if I could just make it to graduation, I could magically transform into the woman I wanted to be. A loft in downtown Los Angeles, my own art gallery, a good-looking husband—they were waiting for me if I could just survive this season.

THE PHONE CALL

I was majoring in Business Administration and Studio Art, so one day after Statistics and Color Theory 101, I made my way to the studio at school. A few hours later, my day's work finished, I began removing the blue, teal, and aqua paint staining my skin and nails with a cloth dipped in turpentine. As I did so, my phone rang. The name *Daddy* flashed across the screen.

"Hey BB," he said in his warm, loving voice. "We just left the doctor and wanted to give you an update on Mom. Are you alone?"

I walked to the corner of the empty studio and sat down on a stool.

"Is Mom okay?" I asked, voice quavering.

A pause hung in the air; the silence felt like an eternity.

"Well, yes, she's going to be fine," he said. "It's just that the doctors discovered something. It's going to be fine. God is in control! I'm taking care of her and we've already set up appointments for next steps—"

Before he could finish his sentence, I asked again, "Is Mom okay?"

There was a hint of weighted reality in my dad's voice. He paused, sighed, and mustered a positive tone of assurance. She was going to be fine, he said again, but the doctors had discovered cancer, and treatment was going to start immediately. The more questions I asked, the more desperate I felt. Not only had she been misdiagnosed for the preceding two years (treated for Graves' disease, treated for Lyme disease, treated for orbital cancer, and labeled a "medical anomaly," which led to experimental treatments), but we had wasted valuable treatment time.

Months before, the doctors had diagnosed my mother with low-grade eye orbital cancer and assured us that, in the grand scheme of things, it was the best cancer to have. Her tumors rested at the end of her eye orbitals, which required facial radiation and oral chemotherapy. "The best cancer to have" seemed the worst way to get your hopes up, but we trusted the doctors and followed the protocols.

There was only one problem: she wasn't getting better; she was getting worse.

Sitting there in the studio, holding the phone to my ear, I felt the air leave my lungs. My father explained that the cancer in her eyes had receded into her central nervous system and was affecting all neurological functions. One cancer had morphed into two; a low-grade diagnosis had become a cancer with terminal potential. A wave of scenes flashed across my mind—my mom's inability to lift her arms, the sudden loss of mobility in her legs, the palsy in her drooping face, the inability to control bladder and bowel functions—and everything suddenly made sense. We had been treating her for the secondary effects of a primary disease. We had been fighting the wrong battle.

My mom's cancer was in her brain.

ON MY KNEES

After I said goodbye to my dad and hung up, I dropped my paintbrushes, grabbed my side bag, and rushed back to my dorm room. Once inside, I collapsed onto my knees and curled myself into a fetal position, sobbing uncontrollably.

I remember every detail of that day—the smell of my dorm room, the sound of students chattering outside on the walkway below, the texture of my woven rug clenched tightly in between my fingers, the taste of the hot tears that streamed down my face and into my mouth as I lay on the floor. Everything.

Trauma seeps into the crevices of the mind as it grows sensory roots. With just one phone call, I awakened to the fact that I had been walking in a desert of self-sufficiency, trusting in the falsehood of *doing, doing, doing*. But doing all the right things didn't help my mother. Treatments, medications, and tests hadn't revealed why she was deteriorating before our eyes. It had taken many misdiagnoses and months of painstaking testing to finally identify her illness with assurance. There were years of medical treatments and tests and doctor visits and medications behind her, and they were all in vain.

The tears stung my eyelids. I hadn't seen this coming. None of us had. I clutched the carpet with all my might as the once-solid ground upon which I stood turned to quicksand.

I screamed into the carpet to muffle the sound. I screamed in fury until my throat was raw. I screamed until I had nothing else to say. Anger grew inside me like a stoked fire. Millions of questions raced through my mind. *Why her, God? Why Mom? How could You do this? Why won't You heal her? When will You hear me? Why are You silent?*

I was confused by the way it seemed a good God allowed bad things to happen to good people. But more than confused, I was angry. Our family had sacrificed everything for the gospel in order to build up the church worldwide.

My parents taught all their children to give generously of their time, money, and love. Although we didn't have much, we always gave what we could. Before my father was a pastor, he was a servant. He woke up before the sun on his one day off each week to gather people from the church we attended and lead them down to Baja Mexico to build orphanages and homes, and to provide impoverished communities with basic needs. He'd later lead international trips deeper into Mexico, to Latin America, and to Japan. He had the most generous heart for those who had grave physical needs as well as deep spiritual needs. How could God allow this illness to strike my father's wife?

While Dad had a global passion for those who didn't know Jesus, Mom loved helping people locally. Whether it was leading the church choir, organizing the homeschool ministry, or volunteering with neighborhood graffiti removal campaigns, she had a heart for her community. She opened our home to neighborhood kids and hosted a "Good News Club" where she taught Bible stories using a felt board and then led all the kids in a craft or activity. My mother gave her life to others; her heart was for the broken. So why did God repay her by giving her cancer? Why didn't He give cancer of the central nervous system to someone who deserved it? At the very least, couldn't He have given cancer to the people who kick little dogs and tell children Santa Claus isn't real?

Just as the Israelites cried out to God for salvation, the fear we face in moments of distress forces us to call upon the One who can save.

Mr. Charles taught us that when the Israelites were enslaved, they cried out to God (Ex. 2:23). He taught us that we, too, had the ability to cry out to a living God who hears us just as He heard the Israelites. I knew I was supposed to cry out to God in my need, but I'd ignored that teaching for so long. Before their exodus, God's chosen people were mistreated, abused, and undervalued from the womb to the tomb. From the depths of their souls, they cried out to God, and He heard them; He understood their pain and remembered His promise to them.

I lay on my dorm floor completely shackled by fear—my own form of enslavement. Like the Israelites, escaping that oppression meant inhabiting my own desert. Like the Israelites, I found myself doubting my ability to survive.

All notions of perfection and poise vanished, and I didn't care if I looked insane and desperate. I *was* insane and desperate. I cried out to God because I didn't have the answers, I couldn't control the situation, and I'd lost my ability to fix, fight, and finagle my way to what I wanted. I screamed into the carpet, clung to the threads with white-knuckled ferocity. Balled up on the floor, I cried out to God from the depths of my soul. I didn't want the desperate life I was living. I didn't care about my idealized notion of perfection. I didn't care about my breakup or my broken heart. In a rasping whisper, I begged God to cover my mother and heal her as only He could.

WINGS AND TASSELS

In the New Testament, Matthew tells the story of a woman who had hemorrhaged for twelve years. Since no one else could heal her, she knew she had nothing to lose by searching for Jesus on the shores of the Sea of Galilee.

Finding Him, she pushed through the crowds. Desperate and alone, she'd spent all her money on remedies, but nothing worked. She wasn't looking for a pat on the back or a hug for affirmation. She had faith Jesus could heal her. Boldly, she pressed through the crowd of people, which according to Levitical Law, was forbidden because of her illness (her hemorrhaging made her impure and therefore required her to remain physically separated from her community). The Law would have branded her unclean, society would have banished her outside the city gates, and the Jewish authorities wouldn't have allowed her to worship in the synagogue (Lev. 15:25).

The woman, however, had nothing left to lose. She had heard of the Messiah who could heal and sought Him out. She said, "If I only touch his cloak, I will be healed" (Matt. 9:21).

But why did she want to touch the tassels of His prayer shawl? This might not mean anything to a non-Jewish person, but given some detective work, I think we could break this down. A tassel would hang on the corners of the prayer shawl and perhaps she remembered this messianic promise: "But for you who revere my name, the sun of righteousness will rise with healing in its wings" (Mal. 4:2 ESV). Perhaps she thought, *If I am to be healed, then it will it be found in his wings* (*tzitziyot*). She showed her belief in Jesus as the Messiah and trusted that He would heal her. At the end of all human resources and logic, she had no choice but to risk her life, to spurn community norms, and to seek healing in Jesus.

Pushing through the crowds, pressing past people, she reached out. The tassels hung low at the bottom of the shawl, so she must have been low, perhaps even on her knees, when she extended her hand toward His garment. At the touch of the hem, she was healed. But following her touch, there was a test. Jesus stopped, scanned the crowd, and asked who had touched Him. I'm sure the disciples were absolutely flabbergasted by the question since they were surrounded by hordes of people. And then, in the midst of the crowd, Jesus saw her. The woman with knee-knocking fear and bold faith caught the eye of the Messiah. "'Take heart, daughter,' he said, 'your faith has healed you.' And instantly the woman was made well" (Matt. 9:22).

THE NAME OF JESUS

As I lay on the floor of my dorm room, I recalled a day years before, a day that was unusually warm as my mom, my twin sister, and I walked out of the post office hand in hand. We discussed things five-year-olds thought important as my mother listened, smiling. Her eight-months-pregnant belly caused her to waddle slightly as we proceeded across the parking lot to the car. But as we neared it, a police siren in the distance interrupted our conversation. It seemed to gain ferocity and draw closer with each passing second. Before we knew it, a young man wearing a navy blue hoodie sprinted past us in a fury, holding a gun.

Police cars pulled into the parking lot, and men in uniforms crawled out of squad cars with military precision, guns in hand. The police screamed at my mom, told her to get us into the car. With superhero strength, my pregnant mother pulled us into the car and flung herself over us, spreading her arms around us like a bird spreading her wings over her young. I looked at my mother with confusion and fear, my eyes wide. We heard gunfire and screaming, but my mother remained calm and quietly whispered over us until the shooting ceased.

"Jesus, Jesus, Jesus, Jesus, Jesus, Jesus, Jesus . . ." She whispered the name of Jesus because it was the only form of strength she could muster. Fortunately, it was the only strength we needed.

Years later, I discovered why she whispered those words over us. Later, I read Romans 10:11–12 and learned that everyone who puts their faith in the name of Jesus will be saved. Later, I experienced the power of the name of Jesus. But in that childhood moment, I clung to my mother, who clung to Jesus.

With that memory in my mind, wrestling with fear and faith, I questioned everything. Was the name of Jesus powerful enough to save my mother? The doctors said she had only a 30 percent chance of surviving and told my father to prepare for her funeral, but I tried to believe God could work with 30 percent. Hadn't He healed the hemorrhaging woman? Weren't the odds stacked against her, too? I sat in the midst of chaos, confused, yet covered by the wings of God. I stood, trembling in fear, and asked Jesus to protect my mother. There was no thunder or lightning, but my soul heard a voice soft and soothing. It whispered to me,

Will you trust Me? Will you have faith that I am good, even if this is bad?

I said nothing, doubting I'd heard anything at all. Wiping the tears from my face, my hands shaking as they dug through my backpack, I found my keys and grabbed my purse.

That night I drove to my parents' house, walked through the front door, and called for my mom. I found her lying on her bed with an expression of confusion and fear, her eyes wide. I sat next to her, spreading my arms around her like a bird protecting its young. Roles reversed, I whispered, "Jesus, Jesus, Jesus, Jesus, Jesus, Jesus, Jesus . . ." over my mother until I could utter no more.

WILL YOU TRUST ME? WILL YOU HAVE FAITH THAT I AM GOOD, EVEN IF THIS IS BAD?

I whispered the name of Jesus over her because it was the only form of strength I could muster. Fortunately, the only thing we could say was the only strength we needed.

Chapter **SIX**

Falling

I've always been a fighter. No matter what's thrown my way, I never stop, never quit. In my mind, I'm like Maximus from *Gladiator* or like Demi Moore in *G.I. Jane.* But the truth is, I'm more like Daniel Ruettiger from the movie *Rudy*, the fifth-string football player from Notre Dame who, despite the odds, worked really hard and played one game in 1974. I'm a hard worker who has fought to keep things together and push things forward. No matter the obstacle, I never give up.

My junior year of high school, I was captain of the track team, and our first meet of the season was a district invitational. I don't know what possessed me, a 5-foot-2-inch Mexi-Rican with no hops (translation: I was short and couldn't jump high), to run hurdles, but in my naiveté I thought I could. The morning air was so cool I could see each breath form puffs of white fog as I got into my starting blocks. To my left was Franisha, and to my right was Aisha, African American sisters with thighs the width and length of Roman columns. I remained tightly poised until the starting gun went off.

At the sound of the gun, I sprinted out onto the track with force and fury. Clearing the first two hurdles and rounding the bend, I was distracted by what looked like a gazelle leaping over the hurdles next to me. I glanced to my left and saw Franisha pass me with ease. Panicked, I felt my cadence being thrown off. Out of rhythm, I couldn't generate the force I needed to clear the next hurdle, and my back knee grazed the top, causing me to land with a wobble. I had to scramble to keep pace.

Without the confidence and velocity I needed, I approached the fourth hurdle, but this time my back knee hit the hurdle, and I fell over it. Determined not to be disqualified, I leapt to my feet and sprinted to the next hurdle, only to fall again. On to the sixth hurdle—I fell. And the seventh. And the eighth. And the ninth. By the time I reached the tenth hurdle with bloody shins and bruised knees, I lifted up my left leg with both of my hands, straddled the hurdle, picked up my right leg, flung it over the hurdle and limped across the finish line as tears ran down my cheeks. To this day, I'm pretty sure I hold the state record for the longest 300-meter hurdle race.

That said, I have always found a way to get back up—whether during a race or in life. But after my mother's diagnosis, I found myself in a season of utter hopelessness. Despite my resilience and commitment to keeping things together, my life was falling apart. I'd tripped over the last hurdle, and I wasn't getting up.

One night, after a full day of classes, I drove home because my younger sister—unable to process my mother's illness and how God could allow bad things to happen to good people—had turned to drugs and alcohol. My father, loving her the best way he knew how, packed two boxes of her things and put them on the front porch, then ordered her out. I tried to console my youngest siblings and explain what was happening to our family, but they were devastated by my mother's diagnosis and by my sister leaving.

After the dust settled, my father, fearful of losing his wife and feeling like a horrible father, fell into a deep depression. I followed suit. In utter helplessness, I cried out to God, lamenting with such pain my chest ached. *What are You doing?* For the first time in my life, my determination was gone; I no longer wanted to get back up and sprint to the next hurdle. I wanted to sit down on the track and complain about everything that was going wrong.

As the days turned into weeks and the weeks turned into months, the slow burn in my chest began to boil. Anger seeped out like beads of sweat, and I couldn't conceal my emotions. The words of Mr. Charles haunted me as I raised an angry fist at God in prayer. "There is a difference between lamenting and complaining," Mr. Charles had explained. "Lamenting is telling God you're sad. Complaining is being angry with God because you're sad." Just as the Israelites grumbled and complained as they wandered across Sinai feeling duped and frustrated, I wandered in my own desert, feeling as lost as they did.

While girls my age were getting married or planning their next getaways to tropical beaches with their trim waistlines, I whispered and complained about what *everyone* else had, who *everyone* else dated, and where *everyone* else was going. One three-day weekend, I was on my way to stay with my mother while my dad was away on a work trip, and I replayed all the conversations with girls in my college dorm.

Girl #1: I'm going to Vegas!
Me: How fun! That will be so great.
Girl #2: I'm spending the day at the beach because school is so exhausting!
Me: Fun. That will be so great.
Girl #3: I'm going on a shopping spree!
Me: That will be so great.
Girl #4: Mani and pedi time!
Me: Great.

I pretended to be happy for them, but inside I was green with envy. I defaulted to my usual coping mechanism and stopped by the grocery store on my way home. I walked aimlessly down the aisles until I found the least healthy, most binge-worthy food. A candy bar, a pint of ice cream, and a bag of chips later, I returned home, plopped on the couch, and drowned my sorrows in food while my mother withered away in the next room. Who needed to hang out with hot guys and have fun when you could chill with Ben & Jerry?

Sucked into social media, a voyeur with an eye on everyone else's life, I inwardly justified my jealousy with self-pity.

How did she get a boyfriend? She's not even nice!
What does he have that I don't? I know I deserved that promotion over him.
They asked her to lead the Bible study? I've been a Christian for longer and she ditches church all the time whenever she feels like it.

I ate and complained, ate and complained. But none of it helped, and the more I ate, the emptier I felt.

THE GOODNESS OF GOD

I can see it now; what my jealousy and complaining ultimately boiled down to was a lack of belief. I doubted what I was raised to believe. I'd heard people declare, *God is good all the time, and all the time God is good!* But was He? Was He a God who cared about me and the copious amounts of ice cream I shoveled down my throat to numb my pain? Did He remember me? Would He keep His promises?

God had worked miracles in the past, but what if He didn't this time? What if my doubting pushed Him away? What if my failure was too much?

I considered Mr. Charles's teachings about the Promised Land, how the Israelites came to the edge of it, saw its goodness with their own eyes, and still didn't believe. I remembered how Moses sent an elite group of spies into the land, how they came back with proof of abundance even though there would be some challenges and obstacles to overcome. But instead of believing the promise of God, that they would live in this land flowing with milk and honey, the people did what came more easily, maybe more naturally—they complained and compared.

With closed eyes and pursed lips, Mr. Charles would shake his head in disbelief, and say, "The children of Israel could have cut their journey by forty years if they had just trusted in the goodness of God." He was right. Theologians estimate that it would have been an eleven-day journey from Egypt to Canaan, the Promised Land, but it took the Israelites forty years to get there because of their unbelief.

I knew I didn't want to wander in the wilderness. I didn't want to remain desperate in the desert. I wanted the freedom I knew God promised to all His children. But I tripped over life's hurdles, and all the complaining, comparing, and overconsumption wasn't helping me get back on my feet.

Chapter **SEVEN**

Retreat

In 2004, short side bangs were all the rage, and I raged with them. Aside from bad hair choices, though, it was also the year my mother invited me to attend her annual church women's retreat. Chemo treatments, radiation, steroids, and painkillers couldn't keep my mom away from this annual gathering. Every year she poured her heart and soul into planning this weekend, a time set apart for women to study God's Word, hear the Holy Spirit, and get away from the demands of life. Every year, I turned down her invitation to attend. But this time I didn't. I was never one for women's ministry (I jokingly referred to it as *women's misery*). Nothing sounded more horrific than spending the weekend with menopausal women bemoaning child rearing and their recent diet fads (at least that's what I thought the weekend encompassed). But when your cancer-ridden, bald-headed mother begs you to attend her favorite church event, you really don't have an option. You just say yes.

I packed my luggage and my best pastor's-kid smile, and drove her to a retreat center in the California desert. I parked my car, and as I walked into the registration center, from a distance, I heard the gaggle of women. I immediately rolled my eyes. I was expecting to find women who were giddy with excitement about leaving their children at home and their inhibitions in the car. And while there were some who fit this stereotype with painful perfection, I was *not* expecting to discover the power of women gathered together in one place seeking one thing—to hear God and be in His presence. It changed everything.

Cultural critic Matthew Arnold wrote, "If there ever comes a time when the women of the world come together purely and simply for the benefit of mankind, it will be a force such as the world has never known." As I sat on a tufted chair in the conference room, maybe I sensed this truth. Music hung in the air like a thick blanket—warm, cozy, comfortable. The worship team sang, and a feeling of calm filled the room. It wasn't mystical or creepy, just simple and holy. The sun had set, and the room was as dark as the inside of a cocoon must be just before the new life inside it breaks free. Something was ready to emerge.

But still, I held back. Maybe it was skepticism. Maybe it was fear. But I could only sit in the back and watch as women were prayed over, worshiped freely and honestly, and exuded a faith that filled every inch of the room. They were old and young, big and small, women whose appearances seemed to melt into each other's with no distinguishing attributes or features as they hugged, prayed, and spoke words of encouragement.

I felt like a tourist in a foreign country, trying to blend in as best I could, but I was unable to speak the language or participate in the cultural exchange of that divine moment. I had been part of that culture before. I had grown up in this faith. Why had I forgotten the language? Why did I feel so foreign?

In this season of God's silence, hope waned as my voice felt raw from petition. No matter how many times I prayed for something to change, no matter how many questions I asked, no matter how I begged, I was met with no response. I wanted nothing more than to hear from God. Jeremiah 33:3 says, "Call to me and I will answer you and tell you great and unsearchable things you do not know," but this felt like a promise for someone else—someone perfect, polished, and pretty. Not me, not desperate, fallible me. Surely God wasn't answering me because I was bad or broken or too bruised to be picked. The refrain of my inner control-freak echoed: *try harder, work faster, be better.* Wash, rinse, repeat.

The truth was, from the moment of Mom's diagnosis, I filled my journals with furious scribbles vacillating from "I believe You can change this situation!" to "Are You even there?" I lay in bed and cried myself to sleep as I heard my mother moan in pain, her body fighting a constant battle with faceless cancer. I begged God for a reprieve. Prayers left my lips like urgent Hail Marys, and I believed that somehow my actions or rote religious rhymes would move God to answer me.

But now in the room full with faith-filled women, I saw that I didn't have to work hard or be better; I simply had to *be.* I just didn't know how.

HOLY SPIRIT

Earlier in the day, before the main evening session, there had been an optional workshop about the Holy Spirit. According to the conference brochure, it was a way for women to learn more about the mysterious third member of the Trinity and discover the natural and supernatural gifts of the Holy Spirit. It was held during a break in the retreat schedule, so while most women opted for a dip in the pool or a cappuccino at the café, I walked into a large room with maroon chairs and sat in a circle of five women. As nervous as I was, I wanted to learn more about the spiritual gifts I'd read about in the Bible and heard various people debate.

At the helm of this Spirit-ship was a white-haired woman with crystal blue eyes and orthopedic walking shoes. I debated rubbing my temples and squinting, feigning the onset of a migraine so I could walk out and avoid judgment. But I felt guilty about reducing the cumulative total of women at the workshop to four, so I stayed. Plus, I was the pastor's daughter, and leaving might make me look like a bad Christian who didn't want to spend extra time brushing up on Jesus-y stuff. To be honest, guilt drove me to stay.

Kathy, the white-haired woman, began talking about the Holy Spirit so personally and intimately, I couldn't help but hold on to every word. What had seemed so foreign and far away began to hit home. The Scriptures she read were a balm to my aching heart. The promises of God in the pages she turned felt like the very Bread of Life my famished soul craved.

> "My Presence will go with you, and I will give you rest." (Ex. 33:14)
>
> "This is what I covenanted with you when you came out of Egypt. And my Spirit remains among you. Do not fear." (Hag. 2:5)
>
> "I will put my Spirit in you and you will live, and I will settle you in your own land. Then you will know that I the Lord have spoken, and I have done it, declares the Lord." (Ezek. 37:14)
>
> ". . . till the Spirit is poured on us from on high, and the desert becomes a fertile field, and the fertile field seems like a forest." (Isa. 32:15)

Her words were like water to my dry, arid soul. I was tired of wandering through the desert, and she promised the Holy Spirit could give me rest (Ex. 33:14). The very presence of God's Spirit was with me, and I didn't have to fear (Hag. 2:5). The Holy Spirit was in me, and I could experience life in a land that was mine to inherit. And when it came to pass, I would know without a doubt that God had done it (Ezek. 37:14). When the Spirit was poured out on me, the desert would become fertile fields, she said, and I so desperately needed to know that the barren areas of my life could see this kind of life again (Isa. 32:15).

I didn't want to just understand or analyze her faith; I wanted to emulate it. Whatever she had, whatever she knew, I wanted it. She was alive and dynamic, and she spoke in a way that displayed her intimate relationship with God. She knew more than just Scriptures or facts; she knew her Savior in the depths of her soul. Her eyes glistened when she spoke of God, her smile revealed her love of Him, and her calm tone was governed by the Prince of Peace. She took us on a journey, helping us to understand the Holy Spirit, how He operated, and why He was important in our lives. She was not heavy-handed with her use of theology, though she unpacked and expounded upon Scriptures about the Trinity. Her focus was on what she knew through experience, and she wanted to demystify the Holy Spirit.

The workshop ended, and as the other women filed out, I lingered for a minute and attempted to swallow the lump in my throat. My hands tightly gripped the sides of my chair as I tried to control my emotions. I closed my eyes and willed myself not to cry. I felt a hand on my shoulder, and when I lifted my head, Kathy's eyes met mine. She asked me if I would like to pray. Unable to form any words, I nodded my head.

Thick and slow and sweet, her prayer oozed out like molasses. She prayed with a confidence and authority unlike anything I had ever heard. She knew things I only vocalized in isolation; she prayed over me, revealing to God things that had been hidden in my heart. The words were not condemning or judging, but honest and raw.

Kathy's words opened and exposed my heart, and I felt like a human onion, reeking more and more as each layer was gently removed. The good Christian girl who attended Sunday school, memorized verses, and saw the miraculous occur in her life had also doubted God's goodness, questioned His existence, and lost faith in biblical promises. It was as if Kathy supernaturally knew each of these secrets, saw every hurdle I tumbled over, and knew of my inability to get back on my feet. She spoke to the microscopic fleck of faith in my soul.

She leaned over mid-prayer, took my hands, and said, "God hears you and knows you love Him."

That was it. That one phrase sent me over the edge, and I began to sob like a teenage girl whose diary had just been read aloud in front of the entire school. My conflicting feelings of relief and embarrassment were soothed as Kathy said over and over, "God hears you and knows how much you love Him."

Beyond the cancer, past the perfectionist complex, after the relationship failures, I realized I had been most overcome by the prospect of crying out to a deity I thought no longer heard me. Deep down, I wanted to believe God was there, that He heard my cries, saw my suffering, and could right all wrongs, but I had been losing hope and faith with every passing day. I had begged God to change me, to intervene in the situations around me, but nothing changed. Like the Israelites of old, I had felt as if my cries fell on deaf ears.

But in that moment, everything seemed to shift. In the stillness, I discovered God had not abandoned me, nor was He ignoring me. I had only to be still and know that He was my God.

CROSSING OVER

Exodus 14 is one of the most dramatic chapters of the Israelites' journey. As the Hebrew refugees fled Egypt, thousands of Egyptian warriors chased after them. The Israelites cried out to Moses and lamented that they'd been led into the desert to die. But Moses declared that they shouldn't be afraid, that the Lord would deliver them. And so it was. That evening, God brought a cloud between the Egyptians and His people so that the Israelites were concealed. He led the escapees to the Red Sea by divine light. There, they reached an apparent impasse.

I know I have a vivid imagination, but this is something out of a soap opera. Can you visualize this scene? Maybe conjuring up drama is easier for me because I grew up watching *telenovelas* with my grandmother. But think about it: this is more intense than *Days of Our Lives* and *The Young and the Restless* combined.

As Pharaoh approached, God's chosen people looked up to see the Egyptian army marching after them. Infants cried, the elderly screamed, men shouted, and women lamented. There is nothing in the chapter that indicates the Israelites were calm, cool, and collected. In fact, Scripture indicates "they were *terrified* and *cried out* to the Lord" (Ex. 14:10, emphasis mine). The people of God were losing their minds, fearful of being slaughtered in the vast desert.

Moses calmed the terrified crowd, motioned with his hands to silence their cries, and in a loud voice declared, "Do not be afraid. Stand firm and you will see the deliverance the Lord will bring you today. The Egyptians you see today you will never see again. The Lord will fight for you; you need only to be still" (Ex. 14:13–14).

"Be still." This is more than just a phrase that was embroidered on my dorm room pillow; it's a powerful instruction, one that's repeated in Psalm 46:10: "Be still, and know that I am God." In the original language, the meaning of *be still* can be translated *to surrender.* When we take a look at Psalm 46 and Exodus 14, we see that both chapters chronicle lamentations and battles, and contain resounding and desperate cries for help. But the apex and anchor of each chapter is the charge to *be still.*

The essence of these Scriptures is clear—the battle is not ours to fight. My mother's cancer was not my struggle; I only needed to surrender to the God who knows all and is in control of all. As Psalm 46 reminds us, God is our refuge and our strength, an ever present help in times of trouble. Because we know He has dominion over everything, just as Moses knew God would fulfill His promise to free His people, we trust God, knowing that He is our rescuer, our deliverer, and our protector.

When we surrender our control, we hand God not only our faith, but also our fear. We don't need to worry about the people who want to silence us, oppress us, or enslave us. We only need to stand firm on the promises of God and discover that He is mighty to save (Zeph. 3:17).

THE SILENCE

The idea of stillness, of silence, frightened me. For months I had been actively filling the silence with action, striving to incite the heavens to part, to make God speak to me. I wanted Him to promise that everything would work out, would be perfect, because I was a good Christian who'd done all the right things, and everything works out for our good according to Romans 8:28, right?

In the years leading up to this moment at the women's retreat, I'd read *The One Year Bible* five times in a row, hoping to read something profound and life-altering. Filling pages of my journal, I penned prayer after prayer. I taught Bible studies, and was a leader in youth-ministry. I was doing all the right things. I could check every box and sign off on all my religious obligations. But there was still something missing; something was off. I was driving on the highway in second gear, getting by but not moving at full speed.

I felt like the mythological phoenix who sang songs in the wilderness, begging to be transformed into something new. I wanted to shed the season I was in like old skin, like a cocoon. I wanted everything in my life to burn away. Nothing seemed to fit. I read Revelation 21:5—*I am making everything new!*—and I clung to those words because I so desperately wanted them to be true at a time when it seemed they couldn't be more false.

My mother's life was still slipping away from us; my younger sister was still on drugs and living dangerously with some friends; I was alone in ministry, love, and life; and I wanted nothing more than to throw in the towel. It was all too much, and God's silence was causing me to doubt His ability to rescue me from the desert.

The desert wilderness isn't only for the wayward and forsaken. The apostle Paul was in the desert for three years and emerged ready to proclaim the truth of the gospel. Moses spent over thirty-eight years in the desert and led God's people through trying times. Abraham was a nomad in the desert. Even Jesus spent forty days in the desert wilderness. And both Job and King David used raw, honest language to describe their desert experiences: "My God, my God, why have you forsaken me? Why are you so far from saving me, from the words of my groaning? O my God, I cry by day, but you do not answer, and by night, but I find no rest" (Ps. 22:1–2 ESV). "I cry to you for help and you do not answer me; I stand, and you only look at me" (Job 30:20 ESV).

Some atheists will tell you God seems silent because He's absent. In the silent suffering seasons, we can be tempted to believe this lie. What we experience as God's absence or distance or silence is just a perception problem, though. The same way we can experience the world as flat even though we're walking on a huge spinning ball, we can experience God as absent or distant even though He is quite near to us.

God wasn't absent or silent or indifferent toward Job or King David. But that's how it felt to them at the time. Nor, in reality, was God silent toward me in my desert days. When I felt most forsaken by God, I wasn't (Heb. 13:5). I was simply called to trust His promise over my perception.

WHY SILENCE?

But why does it need to feel this way? Why the perceived silence? Why can it seem like God is playing hard to get, or like He ignored me when I cried out for help, asking Him to heal my mom for almost three years?

I don't claim to understand all the mysteries of God, but I believe all seasons have a purpose and a reason, even the desert seasons. These are some of the questions that help us frame our faith in seasons of silence, questions that can perhaps help us recognize the beauty of the parched lands and arid winds of the desert:

Why is water so much more refreshing when we're really thirsty?

Why am I almost never satisfied with what I have, but always longing for more?

Why is it that "absence makes the heart grow fonder" but "familiarity breeds contempt"?

Why can the thought of being denied marriage or children or freedom or the fulfillment of some other dream create in us a desperation we didn't previously feel?

Why is the pursuit of achievement often more enjoyable than the achievement itself?

Why do deprivation, adversity, scarcity, and suffering often produce the best character qualities in us while prosperity, ease, and abundance often produce the worst?

There is an invisible pattern in the design of deprivation: deprivation draws out desire. Absence heightens it. And the more heightened the desire, the greater our satisfaction will ultimately be. It is through mourning that we know the joy of comfort (Matt. 5:4). It is the hungry and thirsty who will be satisfied (Matt. 5:6). Longing makes us ask; emptiness makes us seek; silence makes us knock (Luke 11:9). It was at that women's retreat that I began to knock in earnest. It was there that I discovered how hungry I really was. There, I heard the words of a faith-filled woman who said, "God hears you." Believing that truth was the beginning of my path out of the desert.

Chapter **EIGHT**

God Hears

The second night of the retreat, the auditorium was packed for the evening session. Kathy taught from the book of Ephesians about faith and being rooted in God's word. At the end of her teaching, she invited the worship team to lead us in a time of worship and waiting. Waiting, she said, for God to speak to us individually and corporately.

That night I heard women cry out for deliverance, seek God's direction in life, intercede for healing, and believe God for the impossible.

As I watched women go forward for prayer, stand in worship, and cry out to the Lord, I knew something inside me was changing. Women from the church in which I grew up surrounded me. I saw their lives and knew what many of them endured. Some carried emotional scars from affairs; some had lost loved ones; some endured sickness or financial hardship. They had survived their own fires, and they had come out stronger and more beautiful because of their suffering. Their scars testified to their survival. They stood in an act of worshipful defiance. Nothing—not pain or sickness or lack or want—kept them from believing God has been, will be, and is capable of doing impossible things. In a moment of clarity, I realized that the fire I thought was destroying my life was actually refining it.

These women had faced seemingly insurmountable obstacles, just like the Israelites who'd faced the Red Sea. But they'd crossed through their own desert seasons of fear and shame. They'd been delivered just like the Israelites.

IN A MOMENT OF CLARITY, I REALIZED THAT THE FIRE I THOUGHT WAS DESTROYING MY LIFE WAS ACTUALLY REFINING IT.

I considered this passage: "The eyes of the LORD run to and fro throughout the whole earth, to show Himself strong on behalf of those whose heart is loyal to Him" (2 Chron. 16:9 NKJV). God demonstrated His goodness and love to these women, put the wonders of His Word on display for them. And now, His eyes looked upon those who'd seen His goodness. I wanted to see, know, feel, and hear this God. I wanted my own Red Sea deliverance.

Kathy stood next to the worship team and spoke words of truth, words of prophecy, and words of encouragement over the women in that packed auditorium. Her words were familiar, but it felt like she spoke ideas and thoughts straight from heaven, which was confusing to me. I grew up in a theologically conservative household, so I didn't have a good framework for understanding prophetic gifts (WHAT DO PROPHETIC GIFTS EVEN MEAN?!), but Kathy kept bringing everything back to Scripture. She'd say she had a word of knowledge or an exhortation (like Paul spoke about in 1 Corinthians 12—see the appendix for more info on types of gifts), and then she either explained what spiritual gifts were being used or cited a Scripture to support her statement.

She opened her Bible and read Scripture out loud, proclaiming particular promises over these women, for particular people in various situations. She zeroed in on wayward children, health, encouragement, and promises from God. Skeptical by nature, I watched cautiously as women stood for prayer when Kathy asked if a particular verse or prophetic word was for them. In the back of the room, away from most of the women, I thought to myself, *This could all be a joke. How do we know these words of prophecy and promises of healing are for* these *women? Is this even real?*

As I skeptically surveyed the room, I heard Kathy read a verse about healing while placing a hand on her throat. She said she was feeling something in her throat, and that someone needed healing for a specific issue in that area. The woman in front of me leaned toward her friend and said, "God spoke to me, and I heard the same thing."

How was everyone hearing from God, but I was spiritually deaf? Was I a bad Christian? Did I not have faith? Was I being punished? Did my hesitation and skepticism disqualify me from playing with the big kids?

Kathy didn't make the night about her. She never said *she* was going to heal people or pray for people; she knew the body of Christ was stronger than any one individual could ever be. As I sat in that darkened room, I suddenly thought of Tasha Gomez, a girl in my youth group who came to me on a weekly basis asking for prayer for her mother. Week after week, she met me after service to pray for her mother until her mother was finally diagnosed with thyroid cancer and scheduled for surgery the following week. The next thing I knew, I was seeing Tasha's mother stand up on the far side of the auditorium and walk forward for prayer. I had no idea she was at the retreat. *Just a coincidence*, I thought to myself. The woman for whom I had been praying, the one just diagnosed with thyroid cancer, happened to be at the retreat, and coincidentally, God let Kathy in on the secret. The Holy Spirit revealed to Kathy that someone in that room needed specific healing, and she spoke it out in faith.

Just a coincidence. No matter how much I talked myself into believing it was all just random and coincidental, I couldn't help but believe Kathy was right, that God really wanted to speak to us both individually and corporately.

What I didn't know at the time was that the Gomez family was dealing with much more than cancer. Tasha's dad was a closet alcoholic, and her brother was in and out of jail. But Tasha stood alongside her mother and faithfully prayed for something to change in her household. Although Tasha knew God could heal their family, Mrs. Gomez's cancer was the blow they didn't see coming. Tasha's father, devastated by the cancer diagnosis, stopped going to church and abandoned his belief in God.

On the Tuesday following the retreat, I received a phone call from Tasha. The doctors were confused and needed to run more tests. The desperation in her voice and her quavering words reminded me of Kathy at the retreat. In my mind's eye, I traveled back to the auditorium and saw Kathy reach for her throat and pray in faith for healing. I told Tasha I would keep her mom in prayer and see her the next day at youth group.

The next night, Tasha came into our old youth sanctuary

that smelled like teens (a mixture of sugary body sprays, chips, and pubescent body odor) and ran to me. With tears running down her face and wonder in her eyes she said, "B, it's gone! The doctors can't find the cancer! My mom is healed!" She hugged me, and we laughed until we cried and then cried until we laughed.

But more miraculous than Mrs. Gomez's supernatural healing was the supernatural transformation of Tasha's father. For months, her father resented the family for going to church and turned to alcohol to assuage his pain. But after his wife's healing, the same man who denied the existence of God stood in the doorway of the youth sanctuary asking our youth pastor to pray with him. Clutching his jacket in one hand and a child's Precious Moments Bible in the other, he asked if God was powerful enough to heal him too.

I stood there in shock and awe and remembered the night at the retreat. God was on the move. I felt it, I heard it, I knew it, I saw it.

I didn't want to analyze or dissect Kathy's faith; I wanted to emulate it. Whatever she had, whatever she knew, I wanted it. I wanted more of it.

Chapter **NINE**

Holy Spirit

On the final day of the retreat, the prayer team called my mom to the front of the room. One of the leaders pushed her forward in her wheelchair, and the women placed their hands on her body and began to pray. In a beautiful moment of spontaneity, women from all over the auditorium got to their feet, walked to the front where my mother was seated, circled around her, and began to pray out loud. The cadence of their voices filled the room, and I watched as they cried out to God for a miracle. I don't remember what was said, but I remember what I felt: hope.

While I didn't feel a metamorphic shift or hear the audible voice of God, I knew my faith was awakening; something inside me wanted change. The façade was crumbling, the veneer thinning; I needed a transformation. I not only wanted to hear from God again, I wanted to believe His promises. If He could make the old new, the dead alive, and the crooked straight, I wanted to believe He could transform me into the person I was destined to be. As my mom recounted the weekend during our desert drive home, I prayed, *God, work in me.*

The desert sun beat down on us as my mom and I drove home from the retreat, empty land stretching around us into the distance. My mother basked in the work of the weekend and chatted about how happy she was that hundreds of women's lives had been forever impacted. With every ounce of her being, she believed we'd progressed—in big and small ways—into a fresh understanding of who God is and of His immense love for us.

Maybe she was right. I heard, saw, and felt something going on during that gathering of women. There was a smoldering ember that ignited the collective faith, and this fresh faith spiritually awakened even the staunchest of doubters (read: me). Although we didn't have a pillar of fire leading us through the desert like the Israelites, a fire started in my heart.

Jesus said, "The thief does not come except to steal, and to kill, and to destroy. I have come that they may have life, and that they may have it more abundantly" (John 10:10 NKJV). The Message renders it more plainly: "I came so that they can have real and eternal life, more and better life than they ever dreamed of." Better than our best dreams—what a promise. And if we translate this verse from the Greek, it says Jesus came to give us *abundant* life.

Growing up, I didn't have a solid model of abundant life because so many Christians around me lived so many different ways. Some good, Bible-believing Christians lived in constant crisis. Others lived lives of scarcity where everything they had was *just* enough to squeak by. But the saddest Christians were the ones who believed they couldn't have joy. They had *just* enough God to forgive their sins, but not enough to heal them from emotional, physical, or relational pain.

But did Jesus come to give us *barely enough* life? No. Abundant means *more* than more than enough. We see the word *abundant* used in other passages to convey the same thing; it's more than we can think or imagine (Eph. 3:20). I heard this truth many times, but had I experienced it?

Driving home from the retreat with my mom, I nursed a growing understanding of abundant life. We were in the desert both physically and metaphorically. I stared at my mother's head—once full of thick, red hair—her swollen face, and her jaundiced eyes, and I saw abundance. In her most fragile state, she believed in a God who was *more* than more than enough.

She was exhausted and drained, but she possessed *more* than more than enough love, *more* than more than enough joy, and *more* than more than enough hope. She had the abundant presence of a living God. Cancer attacked her body, but could not get to her soul. Her body was deteriorating, but her spirit was growing in strength. In spite of her illness, she wanted to lead the retreat because nothing was going to stop her from creating an experience for women to learn about God and hear from God, even if it took her last breath. And she wasn't the only one with this mindset.

All weekend I had been with women who had real-life pain and real-life issues, but they gave from an internal reservoir that was more than more than enough. Cindy's son was a drug addict. Sylvia's husband suffered from diabetes. Donna's mom was in the hospital. Mary's husband had passed away. And yet these women committed, year after year, to give from a reservoir carved out by pain but filled by God. The Holy Spirit filled what life had hollowed out.

The women with whom I spent that weekend were not

millionaires, but they had more than enough to share. They didn't have mansions, but they offered their homes to people in need. They were busy managing work, families, and busy schedules, but they had more than enough time to give to people who were hurting.

As I was driving home with my mom, thinking about all this, I realized an abundant life is filled with meaning and contentment . . .

filled with design and purpose . . .

filled with happiness and peace . . .

. . . even in the midst of pain, illness, and want.

God wanted the abundant life for me; it was the type of life God created me for, the type of life Jesus came to give. But the abundant life didn't mean I got to skip the desert. It meant I could experience abundance *in the midst* of the desert. I see that now, and know it will be true again. And that promise—the promise of the *more-than-enough* life, even in the desert—is beautiful.

RETURNING HOME

The road, dusty and dry, stretched on in front of us. I was heading back home physically, but I was also heading back home in my heart. I longed to be in a place where God would speak to me. I never doubted He could; I just questioned whether He would. The hope I began to feel in my chest was supernatural. I felt a resurrection coming. I felt like a phoenix rising from the desert ash.

The Israelites were promised a land where milk overflowed

and honey abounded. They would be prosperous and increase in number. The hand of slavery would no longer oppress them. They would live in the land and reap its harvest. Just as Jesus promised the Holy Spirit to us, God promised land to the children of Israel. And when God makes a promise, He doesn't take it back.

I remember Mr. Charles's stories, how he told us of the Israelites who marched day after day, their shoes not wearing thin and their clothes still looking new. But didn't they grow tired? He told us how they circled the same mountain again and again. The desert was their testing ground. If we can survive the harsh circumstances—being lost, questioning provisions, navigating desolate terrain—we can survive even greater tests and moments of discomfort.

What kept the Israelites walking for four decades? What kept them moving forward? I imagine Moses leading the people with a deep, gravelly voice like Russell Crowe in *Gladiator*. Skin made leathery by the sun and hair tousled by the desert winds, he yells, "We've come too far to quit now! We must keep going. We must!" So they pack up camp and follow the pillar of cloud by day and the pillar of fire at night.

The Israelites were guaranteed the Promised Land, and in their desert journey we see the struggle they endured to get there. It was their home, even though they hadn't yet crossed its borders. They knew about it. They knew it would be awesome. They even knew God was going to give it to them. But they hadn't experienced the fullness of it. Over 160 times, the Bible refers to the land as the Israelites', promised to them from generations before.

Over and over from the Old Testament to the New

Testament, we see God make promises and keep promises in His own divine timing. This remains our hope.

During my own journey home, I had to hold to the promise given to me: the Holy Spirit was not only *with* me, but *in* me and *empowering* me to do what God had called me to do. On the road, with my mother in the passenger seat jabbering away, I woke to that truth.

FROM PROMISE TO PRESENCE

Can we geek out for a minute? Or shall I say "Greek out"? (My homeschool humor is just too much to handle, I know.) Scripture mainly uses three Greek words to talk about the Holy Spirit: *para* (alongside), *en* (in), and *epi* (upon). The third verb is my favorite because this is when the Holy Spirit moves from being *alongside* us or *in* us to *upon* us. (Maybe it's my inordinate love of Snuggies and fuzzy blankets, but doesn't that sound AWESOME?)

According to Acts 2, the Holy Spirit moved from a promise to a presence. Jesus promised the Holy Spirit would come, and He did. "When the day of Pentecost came, they [Christ's followers] were all together in one place. Suddenly a sound like the blowing of a violent wind came from heaven and filled the whole house where they were sitting. They saw what seemed to be tongues of fire that separated and came to rest on each of them. All of them were filled with the Holy Spirit and began to speak in other tongues as the Spirit enabled them" (Acts 2:1–4).

Imagine the wonder and reverence present in that room. Can you see it?

I imagine it might have looked a bit like an event we held in college during homecoming weekend. We gathered on the upper lawn of the campus and built a massive bonfire. When I say massive, I'm not being melodramatic. Crates were stacked upon a wooden foundation towering high in the air and lit ablaze while drunken students screamed nonsense about our rival team and the upcoming football game. It was the liberal arts college version of Burning Man (minus the desert, the hippies, and the fire marshal). There were no fire extinguishers and no distinct boundaries to contain the flames. It was open and uncontrolled. It was beyond dangerous and ridiculously scary. Our whole lives, well-intentioned parents had told us not to play with fire. And now, while these same parents paid $45,000 a year for private educations, their children danced wildly around unruly flames. I stood back and stared in awe. Soon enough, though, I approached the flames myself, dancing dangerously close to the warmth of the fire. The flames, although powerful and scary, were also inexplicably beautiful.

I knew the Holy Spirit intellectually, but I didn't know the Holy Spirit intimately. I stood back and watched the flames from afar, but I needed to dance dangerously close to see the Spirit's beauty. When I invited Jesus to be my personal Lord and Savior, I received the Holy Spirit. But looking back on the women's retreat, on the drive home, I see it. That was the moment I asked the power of the Holy Spirit to come *upon* me and empower me to do what God had called me to do: be strong and courageous, keep moving forward, and don't quit in the desert. It was powerful and scary, but it was also beautiful.

The Israelites wandered toward a land promised to them, and I drove to my parents' house. Like the Israelites, I hoped for *new.* Like the Israelites, I wanted my cry to be heard and my heart to be known; I wanted the songs I sang from the depths of my soul to be recognized and acknowledged. But what I needed was a fresh fire. What I needed was to surrender to it.

Part

THREE

Chapter **TEN**

Enter the Fire

Throughout the Old and New Testaments, we find that God has *responded* by, *appeared* in the form of, and been *likened* to fire. In every case, fire is viewed as a symbol of God and His ability to radically change our lives.

God made a covenant with Abraham using the symbol of a smoking fire and blazing torch (Gen. 15:16–17).

Through the fire of the burning bush, Moses received a commission and calling (Ex. 3:2).

Fire protected the Children of Israel during the exodus out of slavery and provided light to guide them (Ex. 13:21).

God displayed His holy purity through fire on Mount Sinai (Ex. 19:18).

God revealed His presence through fire to Shadrach, Meshach, and Abednego (Dan. 3:25).

The Holy Spirit transformed and empowered Jesus' followers in the form of fire on the day of Pentecost (Acts 2:3).

Fire was alive and well in my life during the diagnosis of Mom's illness, breakup with my ex, college graduation, and subsequent unemployment. Did this mean God was at work?

Or did this mean I was paying penance for something I had done or some mistake I had made?

In the firefighting community, there is a phrase to express a critical moment in the beginning stage of a fire. This moment occurs when the temperature gets to a certain level, and everything combustible in a room spontaneously bursts into flames, spreading the fire instantaneously. This is called the "flashpoint." In those days, the temperature of every area of my life had simultaneously reached a level of combustion. It started to feel like a scene from the movie *Backdraft* or *Ladder 49*. Fire seemed to be everywhere. It was relational. Physical. Familial. Financial. Spiritual. There was heat on all fronts, and as I reached my flashpoint, everything I ever wanted burned down around me. As I watched my life blazing, I was left with a choice: walk away from the flames, or walk into them.

ALONE

From conception I had a partner, a twin sister. We were born one minute apart. From the moment of my first breath, I had someone with whom I could laugh and cry. My twin, Jasmine Star, bore not just my resemblance, but my story.

Photo albums and accounts from my parents testify to the instant bond between us. Cassette tape recordings of toddler chipmunk voices reveal a language only we shared. We made odd-sounding noises, laughed uncontrollably at our own gibberish, and babbled to each other from our cribs as we fell asleep.

For my entire life, I had someone by my side who understood my feelings before I could put them into words. Likewise, with a simple glance, I knew what she was thinking, feeling, or needing. I didn't just have a soul mate in my sister; I had a womb mate. When you are created at the same time, in the same place, at the same moment, you are never alone. Or at least that's what you think.

But here I was at her wedding reception, seeing Jasmine happier than she'd ever been. In the arms of her husband, she danced under the light of the moon as the sound of waves crashed on the Hawaiian sand beneath us from the hotel balcony.

The wedding was beautiful. Jasmine married her best friend, and I watched with sheer joy as they promised to love each other unconditionally. They made their vows, forsook all others, and were joined in holy matrimony. And now, they were hand in hand, her husband leading her in a dance the way he would lead her through life, in times of both joy and trouble.

My heart was happy, but my soul was sad. She'd found her soul mate, but I'd lost my womb mate. I had walked through deserts and rough terrain with her, but now I was at a point where I had to release her into the arms of someone else.

Jasmine packed up the life we shared and prepared to move out. We sat on our bed and divided our property in half. Half of the clothes we shared, half of the makeup we'd accumulated, half of the shoes we'd bought. Half of my heart felt like it was stuffed into boxes that day.

My womb mate was leaving me to become one with someone else. It was a marriage for her, but a divorce for me. I smiled and hugged her, but I wanted to go back in time, reach out to her crib again, utter words that only she could understand, and ask her not to leave me. I was afraid and alone and ashamed that I couldn't fully celebrate her happiness.

The day we returned home from her wedding, I lay in my room and sobbed uncontrollably. While Jasmine's life was moving forward, I remained at home with a dying mother and failed dating life. My bed felt extra big and my soul extra empty. For the first time, I felt utterly alone. Yes, I had been in the desert for some time, but at least I was walking in barren lands with someone who was on a similar journey. From my mother's diagnosis, to her treatment, to nursing her through the side effects, to the fear of losing her, Jasmine was by my side.

I hailed from a large family (we're Latino—what do you expect?) and attended a large church, but after my sister moved away, I couldn't shake the loneliness I felt. I'd walk into a room filled with people and still feel alone. The smiles and laughs were genuine, but left me feeling empty.

My longing for love and acceptance was painful. Still recovering from three years of degrading dysfunction in my last dating relationship, I became the single friend who attended weddings *sans* a date, RSVPing without a plus-one, and praying no one would ask why I was *still* single. During the ceremonies, I heard vows of "for better or worse, until death do we part" and prayed it would all hurry up so I could make my way to the reception, where I'd drown my jealousy in toothpicked hors d'oeuvres and watery punch.

Everyone was in a season of change—everyone, it seemed, except me. The invitations arriving in the mail progressed from college graduations to bachelorette weekends to weddings and eventually to baby showers. Life was moving forward for everyone else, but I remained alone. It was a never-ending season of dinners for one, solo trips to the movies, and wondering when I'd find someone to love me. Someone to love *all* of me, someone to hold my hand in the midst of the desert and whisper in my ear, *This, too, shall pass*.

It was an endless slog, my own version of a forty-year journey. If I'd had my own personal Moses, I might have asked the same question the Israelites did: *When will this change?* You know this question, don't you? In the moments of loneliness, in the moments of pain, in the moments of loss, in the moments of silence, in the moments of walking in circles in the desert, it's hard not to ask, *When will this change? When will I change? Will it change?*

FLASHPOINT

It was Valentine's Day weekend. I was working as a makeup artist for special events, and I was booked for a wedding in my ex-boyfriend's hometown (yes, *that* ex). For years, we'd been on-again off-again, and as I drove home from the wedding in a new BMW convertible (that I couldn't afford—quarter-life crisis, anyone?), I couldn't shake the thought of him. Maybe it was because I was near the city where we shared so many memories. Maybe the wedding had put me in a sentimental mood. I can't be sure of the reason, but I picked up my cell phone and dialed his number.

In a moment of strength two months earlier, I had turned down his invitation to go on a date and try to reconcile our relationship. It was Christmas, and I knew he was back from touring with his band. (Note: *never* date a musician. I kid, I kid.) I assumed he wanted someone to kiss under the mistletoe and parade around at holiday functions, but even so, he was hard to resist. My loneliness was palpable, but I somehow managed to eke out a "no."

Driving down the highway that night, though, I succumbed to my weakness. I tapped out his phone number, resenting the fact that I still had it memorized. Not wanting to return home to the sickness, loneliness, and listlessness I faced, I reached out to him as a means of escape. While his phone rang, I daydreamed. Maybe it would work out this time. Maybe we would complete each other's sentences and laugh at inside jokes and grow old on our wraparound porch while we reminisced about the time we broke up.

Or maybe I'd watched *The Notebook* one too many times.

The phone rang for so long, I expected to get his voicemail. But then he finally answered, and his deep voice sounded safe and known and usual. It was all the things I longed for but didn't have. I wanted to talk to someone who would hear me. I wanted to talk to someone who would talk back. I used God's silence as an excuse to find solace in my own way, to pacify my fears of being unwanted, alone, and not enough.

He was happy. I heard it in his voice. Everything inside me wanted to believe that the happiness I heard coming through the phone was because I had called. I asked how he was doing. "Fantastic," he replied. He sounded joyful. "Life is changing for the better, and I'm finally at the place where I am truly excited." This was an answer to prayer! The manic-depressive nature that made him a wonderful musician was also the pressure point in our relationship. He was finally settling into a rhythm of health, and I was so excited.

"Wow! What on earth is going on?" I asked with a coquettish giggle.

"I'm getting married!" he said.

All the air escaped my lungs, and I felt faint. I was driving eighty-five miles per hour on the freeway, and I had to pull over. Before I could gather my thoughts, it was as if an extraterrestrial voice rose from within me and responded, "Oh greaaaaat. How greaaaat." It was said in the way my Southern college friends had taught me when you really are trying hard to be nice, but you don't mean it, with wide eyes, a large smile, and all those extra syllables.

I repeated myself. "Isn't that greaaaaat? How greaaaaat is that?"

He began talking, but I heard nothing. I tried desperately to make sense of the timeline—just two months earlier he was trying to repair our relationship. I tried to understand how he could be engaged when just two months earlier, he was telling me he loved me. I tried to process the news. The man I'd loved for three years was marrying someone else—and just two months after he asked me to take him back.

Cars zoomed past at breakneck speed while I sat static. It was a physical picture of the metaphoric state of my life. His voice began to fade in when I heard my name.

"Bianca? Are you there?" He sounded concerned.

"Oh yes, I'm still here. I must've gone through a dead zone. I'm driving. Well, listen, I don't want to lose you again, so I'll let you go. But congratulations on getting engaged. That's so greaaaaat."

I said goodbye in a way that would make a Texas beauty queen proud, and hung up the phone. In complete silence, I started the car, placed my hands on the steering wheel, and stared out my front window. And then I lost it. With every ounce of anger in me, I screamed aloud. I had the steering wheel in a death grip. White-knuckled, no doubt red-faced, and tasting salty tears pouring down my cheeks, I lost it.

"Where are You?

Do You hear me?

WHERE ARE YOU?

Answer me, God! *Answer me, please.*"

This was the moment of combustion, my flashpoint. It wasn't his news or the inherent rejection, but rather the culmination of my feelings of loss and loneliness. I felt like everything I once had was finally, completely incinerated—my sister was gone, my mother was dying, my ex-boyfriend was getting married. I sobbed uncontrollably until the road in front of me was a blur. I screamed until my voice was gone. I cried until there were no more tears. Then I put my car in drive and headed home in silence. There was nothing more to say.

Chapter **ELEVEN**

Crying Out

A famous saying goes, "When you get to the end of your rope, tie a knot and hold on." But I felt like I had no more rope. Left with nowhere else to turn, I went back to a Bible verse Mr. Charles asked me to memorize because it was the only thing that came to mind. "Call to Me, and I will answer you, and show you great and mighty things, which you do not know" (Jer. 33:3 NKJV).

As I sat in my car and screamed, "WHERE ARE YOU? God, can You hear me?" I felt like the last shred of hope in my heart was flopping around helplessly like a fish out of water. At decibels I didn't know humanly possible, I found myself screaming at God and begging Him to stop hiding from me. Theologically, I knew God would right every wrong, but realistically, I questioned His power because of His apparent absence.

I felt hopeless. Eventually, even weeping felt like a waste of emotion, and I had no energy to mourn anymore. I screamed at God, shouted at the top of my lungs, *How could You allow me to be in this place? Where are You?* The last thing I wanted to do was calmly pray.

But there are characters peppered throughout the Bible who felt the same way I did, who lamented and cried out to God, like Job, David, Hannah, and Elijah. When they cried out, shouted their questions to God, didn't God show up? Didn't He demonstrate His loving care and powerful hand of protection?

QARA

Crying out is a humble reminder that we need God every moment of every day. The Bible makes a clear distinction between *prayer* and *crying out*. The children of Israel cried out to be free from bondage and the Lord rescued them (Ex. 3:7). David cried out for healing and God spared his life (Ps. 30:2). Later, in a moment of desperate need, David fled from Saul to a cave and penned a psalm, believing he would be vindicated after crying out to God (Ps. 57:2).

God's word is full of promises for those why cry out to Him. But my favorite is God's promise to Jeremiah, that the Lord gives wisdom to His people in times of perplexity and confusion (Jer. 33:3). God's promise to Jeremiah all those years ago is true for us today. The Creator of the universe wants an intimate, loving relationship with the people He created. A vital component of our relationship is voicing aloud our need for Him.

At the lowest point in my life, I still wrestled with a common theological question: If God knows all—including my heart and mind—why do I have to express myself aloud to Him? Why do I have to cry out? Why do I have to pray? And here's what I found. Yes, God knows our hearts and hears the faintest whisper for help rising from the deepest places in our spirits. But when we're desperate enough to cry out, we are humbled. And when we're humbled enough, something happens—God responds with saving power.

Several verses in Scripture speak very clearly about this exact thing. And even though I felt like I was losing my mind on the side of the freeway that February day, I found some ancestors in the Bible who were just as frustrated as I was. Several Hebrew words describe crying out, but one specific verb, *qara,* connotes the action of calling or crying out loud. *Qara* is used in Jeremiah 33:3 when the Lord says, "Call to Me, and I will answer you, and show you great and mighty things, which you do not know" (NKJV).

During this season of God's silence, I read the Psalms and felt as if David were my long-lost mentor. Deep in the pages of Scriptures, buried in the annals of history, lived a shepherd boy turned war hero turned superstar turned fugitive who penned painful words of loneliness, prophecy, and promise. He used *qara* frequently, and I believe it was because he knew crying out came before worship. "*Call* upon Me in the day of trouble," he wrote in Psalm 50:15, "I will deliver you, and you shall glorify Me" (NKJV, emphasis mine). David penned this in Psalm 145:18: "The Lord is near to all those who *call* upon Him, to all who *call* upon Him in truth" (NKJV, emphasis mine).

The New Testament writers affirm this crying out too. Paul shows us that crying out is a natural impulse planted in our hearts by the Holy Spirit within us. "Because you are sons," Paul teaches in the New Testament, "God has sent forth the

Spirit of His Son into your hearts, crying out, 'Abba, Father!'" (Gal. 4:6 NKJV). The original word used here for *crying out* is a strong one, usually translated as "shouting." So if I could paraphrase this, I'd say the Holy Spirit is at work within us to prompt a shout to God, our Daddy.

As a father of five, my dad could recognize each of his children's cries. Even from a different room and out of sight, the moment he heard a cry, he could identify who was crying and the severity of the situation. All my siblings still call him for advice, affection, and attention, and he loves it. In the same way, I chose to believe God would respond to me, His earthly daughter, and recognize my cries for help from the side of the highway. Maybe, just maybe, the louder I cried, the more likely He was to respond.

Crying out to the air, pounding my steering wheel like a boxer fighting my own shadow, I believed—I *chose* to believe—God heard me.

Scripture gives us an open invitation to shout aloud, to ask God to respond. And that day, in my car alone, I did, quite literally.

Up until this flashpoint, I was unable to admit to anyone that I needed help. While I was trying desperately to keep my life together, the idea of confessing my needs aloud or asking for help was humiliating. From playground mockery to academic humiliation, I had never wanted to be in a position where I needed assistance; I never wanted to be vulnerable again.

My sophomore year of college, I took a political science course on the Cold War. Never in my academic career had I struggled so much to retain or process information as I did in

Dr. MacIssac's class. The entire semester I powered through, creating color-coded notes and hosting massive study sessions, all to no avail. The day of the final exam, I found myself in his office sobbing uncontrollably because I was sure I had failed. Passing me a tissue, he asked why I hadn't come to him with my struggles earlier. The confession came out as uncontrollably as my tears. I explained that I was too embarrassed to ask for help, because everyone would know I was stupid.

I'd spent my whole life in hiding, finding it too difficult to cry out for help in times of trouble. I preferred to endure on my own in the face of insurmountable odds, to try to overcome, so I could raise my hands like a victor, believing, *I did it!* But doesn't God work differently? Doesn't He want us to come to the conclusion, *God did it!* In acknowledging our weakness, the way I did in front of Dr. MacIssac, we experience God's strength and grace in the face of our lack. (I ended up finishing the course strong because I was given the opportunity to supplement my grade by writing an extra credit paper.)

It takes humility to cry out to God in our distress. And humility before the living God is exactly what we need for transformation to occur.

WORSHIP IN THE WILDERNESS

During desert seasons and moments of silence, God is with us. When the Israelites wandered in their own literal desert season for forty years, their clothes didn't wear thin, nor did their shoes break. The Lord provided food, and water flowed. According to chapter 13 of Exodus, God's presence was with them as a cloud during the day and a pillar of fire at night (vv. 21–22).

Theologians call this phenomenon a theophany, the presence or appearance of God. We see this in Exodus 19:9, when the descent of the Lord is marked by a thick cloud.

When the Israelites wandered in confusion, the pillar of cloud led them. When the Egyptians followed them, the pillar of cloud hid them. When darkness fell, the pillar of fire guided them (Ex. 13).

In our moments of confusion, fear, loss, and darkness, we have a God whose presence is with us, who answers us when we cry out. And when He responds, when He shows up in the desert, we have one job: worship God. As we read in Exodus 7:16, Moses declared to Pharaoh, "The LORD, the God of the Hebrews, has sent me to say to you, 'Let my people go, so that they may *worship me in the wilderness*'" (emphasis mine).

This one small sentence is easy to overlook, but it's an important one.

The purpose of the Israelites' deliverance was not simply their emancipation from slavery; it was to lead them into deeper worship of the Lord. Likewise, God doesn't lead us out of bondage and into our own deserts simply for the sake of our own freedom. He leads us into the desert that we might learn to worship Him. And here's the truth—we cannot worship God for the gifts of freedom and salvation without having known captivity and desolation first. When we know the cost of our freedom, it drives our worship. True worship almost always happens in the desert wilderness, and praise is almost always the answer to a plea that rises up in us while we are in the desert.

Looking back, I can see that some of my deepest and most

heartfelt prayers, laments, and sob-fests came from my desert of loneliness.

LEARNING THE LESSON

When you're a twin, being alone not only feels foreign; it feels like a punishment. Attending parties, gatherings, and even church alone was confusing. I was surrounded by people, yet still felt incredibly lonely. I didn't know how to worship in this wilderness of solitude and isolation.

For three years, my coworker, Allison, with whom I ran, swam, and worked out, was single. We both served in youth ministry and spent most of our weeks planning events that consumed our weekends. We shared an office, a ministry, and a passion. We were diametrically different, but vocation made us coworkers, and our open hearts made us friends.

I wore high heels and makeup to work every day. Allison wore flip-flops and didn't even tweeze her eyebrows. She was punctual and responsible. I was spontaneous and never had parents sign student release forms. By her own admission, she was reserved and skeptical by nature. I talked to everyone (even those who didn't want to converse) and inevitably hugged them when I finished emotionally vomiting. We were so different.

Then Allison met a wonderful man. A few months later, they were engaged. Slowly our time together waned as she busied herself with wedding plans. She turned in her resignation, got married, and moved to the other side of the world with her new husband. Allison was just one more girl whose life was moving forward while I circled the same mountains in the same desert in the same season of loneliness.

But this time, instead of *crying* on my bed about being alone, I *cried out* to the One who could meet me in my aloneness. I discovered God in the desert of my life when I turned to Him to satisfy my thirst. As David urged his readers, as Kathy taught me, as Mr. Charles reminded me, I called out to God because only He could hear and heal. Only He could change me in the midst of the pain. Only He could teach me how to worship in the desert.

As I scour the pages of Scriptures, the stories in the Bible show me that desert longings are best expressed through the language of lament, through crying out. The barrenness of the wilderness, the perceived desolation, the loneliness that is only experienced in the desert leads us either toward God and His presence, or into self-reliance, self-loathing, or self-worship. In short, we walk into worship or away from it. This is the pivotal decision: we can cry out and then worship in our Promised Land, or curse God and walk further into the wilderness of our own despair.

I consider the stories of the Israelites. In the desert, their thirst was quenched with water miraculously provided from a rock (Ex. 17; Num. 20). In the desert, when they were under constant threat of attack, God protected them. Moses assured them, "The Lord will fight for you; you need only to be still" (Ex. 14:14). In these and countless other instances, God demonstrated how He responds when His people cry out. He showed them His worth.

And His worth is at the core of right worship. In fact, the word *worship* is derived from worth-ship. We worship

God because of His infinite worth. Through their wilderness cries, the children of Israel discovered that above all others, God is worthy of our praise.

Years later and cultures removed, my proverbial wilderness is where I discovered that above all else, God is worthy. He was the Father the Israelites wanted. He was the provider they needed. He was the mighty One without whose protection they would have disappeared in the desert sands. God began filling the empty parts of my soul and meeting the needs of my heart. I slowly discovered worship doesn't simply occur because God demands it, but because we recognize He's worth it.

The wilderness is still the place where God's people learn to worship. The desolation and emptiness we experience show us our need for the palpable presence of God. More than the perfect boyfriend, the ideal body, the corner office, or validation from the other people in our lives, we need to experience the God who is with us in the driest of seasons. Only He can provide the necessities when we cry out in the desert, and we will worship in the land of His provision.

Jesus said **He** is the bread of life and living water. We need spiritual "bread" every bit as much as the Israelites needed manna in the wilderness. (Note: God wouldn't call Himself the BREAD of Life if He didn't want us eating carbohydrates! Oh no, Paleo. I'm done with you.) Our deepest thirst for living water is just as intense as the Israelites' thirst for physical water. If you find yourself in the wilderness, realize that though you may not feel like it at the moment, you are in the very place where true worship can happen. Like the Israelites, you are on the edge of a very promising place.

How do I know? I experienced it.

Chapter **TWELVE**

Surrender

After my freeway meltdown, I was at a point of capitulation and desperation. I lay on my bed in the quiet of my room (the room in my parents' house that was mine in high school, and which I moved back into as an adult) and cried. This was my white flag moment, my moment of surrender. The tears streaming down my face were the only outward sign of emotion. This wasn't my regular emotional breakdown. This was different. I didn't wail or wince; I didn't kick or scream. I literally opened my hands and surrendered to God in silence.

I'd been through months of diet pills, an expensive car purchase, countless Bible studies, vacations, serving at church, and retail therapy; nothing healed my hurt and confusion. Nothing brought me peace. Nothing provided reprieve or hope or balance in the way I thought it would. I created gods I thought could rescue me from my loneliness, but my attempts at *healing* kept coming up empty and draining any hope (and money) I had.

Now, for the first time, I felt like the change I wanted was happening. It wasn't what I expected or how I wanted it to happen, but I knew God was doing it, even if I didn't like *how* He was doing it.

My moment of surrender should have come as no surprise. Throughout the Bible, in both the Old and New Testaments, situations that seem far beyond salvaging become the impetus for new and greater life.

Jonah was in the belly of a fish, and when he was spewed out, he obeyed God and went to preach to a straying Nineveh.

Abraham took Isaac up a mountain to be sacrificed and trusted that God would fulfill His promise that Abraham would become the father of many nations, even though He'd called Abraham to slay his firstborn.

Paul and Silas experienced a massive earthquake in prison; they lived through the catastrophe, and ushered in salvation and revival to the Roman jail guard and his entire family.

> WHAT LOOKS LIKE IMPENDING DEATH OR UTTER DESPAIR SIGNIFIES THE BEGINNING OF A RESCUE, A DEMONSTRATION OF RESURRECTION, OR THE IMPETUS FOR REVIVAL.

What looks like impending death or utter despair signifies the beginning of a rescue, a demonstration of resurrection, or the impetus for revival. We simply must, like Jesus crying out in the garden of Gethsemane, remain in the process.

DESERT BRAIN

Have you heard the stories of people found wandering in the desert? They are parched, dry, and covered with sand. I've heard they often look insane, and sometimes—depending on how long they have been wandering—actually go insane. They see mirages. They imagine water where there is none.

Spiritual deserts do that to us sometimes too. We don't always think clearly or make the best decisions, and sometimes we see our own spiritual mirages, things that don't really exist. We see comfort where there is none, create imitation gods to satiate our desires. We are prone to say yes to things when we should say no.

The children of Israel suffered from a classic case of what I call "Desert Brain." It hasn't been medically diagnosed, but the symptoms include:

- Chronic forgetfulness of God's past provision
- Constant complaining and grumbling about God, despite His provision
- Neglecting to honor and acknowledge the goodness of God
- Forging man-made saviors and gods to satiate personal desires

Doesn't this describe the children of Israel in Exodus 32? A few chapters earlier, Moses talked to his people, letting them know God wanted them to purify themselves because He was going to give them a message. A thick layer of smoke shrouded the mountain as God descended and hovered over in the form of fire. The ground shook like the San Andreas Fault line as increasingly loud trumpets blasted. The awe must have been palpable as the Israelites watched Moses ascend the mountain and step into the presence of God while they waited at the base. When Moses returned, he came bearing commands for the Israelites to obey, and they agreed.

Moses was summoned to the mountain again, but this time he stayed a lot longer. Fire blistered at the top of the mountain as smoke billowed below. But while Moses communed with God, the people down the mountain felt alone and abandoned. Day after day, they wait for Moses, but he didn't return. Moses's absence and the seeming silence of God was a breeding ground for their control and self-indulgence to kick in.

Instead of remembering how God always showed up for them—sending plagues, guiding their exodus out of slavery, parting the Red Sea, and providing food and water in the desert—the Israelites had chronic amnesia on their journey to the Promised Land. They constantly forgot what God had done for them and blatantly ignored His commands.

The people grew tired of waiting for Moses to come down from Mount Sinai. God's silence felt like absence, and Israelites impatience prompted them to create their own gods. Aaron, Moses' brother, caved in to the complaining of the Israelites. Under his leadership, the people made a golden calf, which they worshiped and—get this—claimed was the god that led them out of Egypt (Ex. 32:4).

It's true—these Israelites lost their minds! But was I so different from them in my own desert wandering?

LETTING GO OF THE IDOLS

Looking back, I suppose I wasn't even aware of how ridiculous I was acting. I spent money on clothes and shoes as a coping mechanism to help me deal with my issues of value and worth. I bought a BMW convertible because I wanted something—anything—to make me feel like I could go farther and faster in life. And I had braids with hair extensions because, well, I obviously had no clue what I was doing with my hair.

I unknowingly set up my own gods and demigods to deal with the silence and supposed inaction of God. And I couldn't see my sin or recognize my own idolatry. Unlike the children of Israel I didn't craft a calf out of gold, but I worshiped designer labels and status symbols, the way I should have been worshiping God. All the while, I kept telling myself I was doing everything "right." I was reading my Bible! I was praying! I was going to church! I wasn't like *those* people! I frequently used exclamation points!

Ultimately, I believed I was less guilty than those who had gone before me. I compared my small idols to the Israelites' big idols. But idols are idols. I compared my small sin to their big sin. But sin is sin. I didn't want to see myself like the idolatrous Israelites, but the truth is, I was no different.

HISTORY REPEATS

Years after the Israelites were delivered from their desert, a prophet named Elijah rose up among them. In those days, the people of Israel followed in their predecessors' footsteps, and although they weren't endlessly circling Mount Sinai like the Israelites of Exodus, they were living in their own spiritual desert, doing their own thing and making poor decisions. They'd even slid back into their old habit of idolatry. (Not another golden calf situation, right, guys?) This time, the Israelites were under the reign of King Ahab and his wife, Jezebel, who were wicked to the core. Elijah, a loud-mouthed prophet, spoke out against the worship of their false gods and warned everyone to stop their stupidity.

In his flamboyant and faith-filled fervor, Elijah prayed that God would withhold rain from the land. Hold on, let's get this: *he asked God to keep the water tap from heaven turned off until people's hearts were changed.* For three-and-half years, his prayers were answered with a ban on liquid goodness (AKA water).

Let's do some basic math. According to my number crunching, that meant no rain for roughly 1,275 days! Livestock died, vegetation withered, the land dried up in a drought.

At the end of these three desert years, God sent Elijah to call all the Israelites and their wicked king to Mount Carmel to settle once and for all the question of the one true God. It was a showdown of sorts. As exciting as a rap battle or dance off would have been, the deciding factor would be which god answered by fire.

FLASHPOINT

If God had a résumé, I'm pretty sure it would include "trained in the art of flamethrowing." In Exodus, He lit up a bush and led people like an ever-moving campfire by night. As we will see in 1 Kings, He threw down some heat and lit up some barbecue in order for Elijah to demonstrate His power. As Elijah had promised, the Lord showed himself to be the one true God. As my mother says, when things need to get awakened, God will sometimes light a fire under our butts to get us moving.

I should mention a few details here. God told Elijah that if he were to confront the king, He would bring rain to the land. One small detail: AHAB HATED ELIJAH. One big detail: JEZEBEL HATED ELIJAH MORE THAN AHAB. Considering where Elijah stood with the royal family, God's command could very well have been a death sentence, but Elijah boldly called out to King Ahab to a dance off . . . wait . . . I mean face off at Mount Carmel.

Picture the scene. All the Israelites came from near and far, all the prophets rolled up, and King Ahab spoke to Elijah. There was a battle of words. Some smack talk was exchanged. Ahab called Elijah a troublemaker. Elijah shot back a retort and named Ahab's daddy and family as the cause of trouble for the nation. You know it gets serious when you start talking about family! Elijah told the king that God had brought the drought because the people had turned from the one true God and worshiped Baal. And he didn't stop there. All the 850 prophets of Baal and Asherah who ate at the royal table, who'd condoned Ahab's sin, were called out too.

The king stepped to Elijah, but Elijah didn't back down. He called out King Ahab to back up the smack he'd been talking. Elijah just laid it down. This was the battle to trump all battles. The Capulets and the Montagues, the Jets and the Sharks, the Hatfields and the McCoys—none of them could rival the drama that went down.

Elijah asked everyone on the mountain to commit, to choose which god they would serve. He challenged the prophets of Baal, asked them to place a bull on the altar and to pray for Baal to set fire to the bull. The prophets did as they were told, then wailed and cried out, but nothing happened. They shouted and cut themselves to gain the attention and favor of Baal, but no fire fell.

Elijah, tired of waiting, began to taunt and make fun of the prophets. "Shout louder! He's a god, so maybe he's busy." The insults grew increasingly heated, and, as some theologians interpret it, Elijah asked if Baal hadn't answered because he was busy in the bathroom (1 Kings 18:27 ERV). OH NO, HE DIDN'T!

Yes, he did.

There was no barbecue for Team Baal. Not even a spark fell from above, and now it was time for God to move. On the surface, the odds were not in Elijah's favor. Consider what he was up against:

- A king and queen who despised Elijah and wanted him dead
- 850 false prophets
- Slim chances of survival if God didn't show up in fire
- No proof that God had ever done what Elijah was expecting Him to do

Undeterred, Elijah trusted God. And when it was his turn to call for fire, he even upped the ante. Elijah rebuilt God's altar, dug a trench around it, and prepared a bull to lay across the altar. Then he drenched everything in water four times over. Why the water? Simple. If the sacrifice caught fire, no one could claim happenstance or coincidence. It would show that an all-powerful God had done what no other god could do.

And then, in his grand moment, with all the prophets of Baal pitted against a single man of God, Elijah cried out to the Lord on behalf of the people of Israel. God would answer His prophet in this desert showdown, and by His power the people would see His greatness. And His greatness they definitely saw. At Elijah's cry, God rained fire from heaven upon the altar, and the flames not only consumed the sacrifice but the wood, the altar, and the dust around it. After seeing this amazing display, the people fell on their knees and proclaimed, "The Lord—he is God! Yes, the Lord is God!" (1 Kings 18:39 NLT). As revival broke out in the land, the dams of heaven broke too. Much-needed rain poured down on the dusty soil, bringing a new season of fruitfulness to a dead land.

On that mountain Elijah called God's people by name. "Your name shall be Israel," he called to them (v. 31). This moment, while less dramatic than raining fire, is much too powerful to gloss over. Elijah reminded the Israelites of their status as God's chosen. This message is as important for us today as it was in the days of Elijah, because while the enemy knows our name, he calls us by our sin. **God knows our sin, but calls us by our name.** Sometimes a reminder of who we *are* is stronger than a rebuke of what we are *not*.

Sometimes we will be forced to choose our way or God's way. Will we fight for control, dance at the altars of our own Baals, or will we cry out and surrender to deliverance? Will we put our works on the altar and let them be consumed by fire? How will we respond?

In desert seasons, or when we've simply lost our way, we are susceptible to forgetting about the power and might of our God and following the desires of our own hearts. The children of Israel were. I was. Worse, we are susceptible to worshiping things that replace God in our lives.

Just as God sent Elijah to urge the Israelites to surrender and turn away from their gods, He still sends people to remind His children to surrender and let go of gods who can't rescue, respond, or react. Just as the children of Israel had a spiritual history and witnessed God do mighty things, so did I.

At times God has to get our attention in the desert before He can speak to us in the fire of the Promised Land. Elijah's story shows us that suffering of the people can be good, so long as it leads to the fire of spiritual revival.

Looking back, I believe my mom was a catalyst for change rather than a victim of circumstance. I saw the impact she had on the lives of so many people, and I started to believe her life—like Elijah's—was a vehicle for revealing the power and speaking out the promises of God. Even if it meant suffering, she was going to live her life bringing glory to God.

I wasn't on Mount Carmel, I didn't see Elijah, and the prophets of Baal were long gone, but God was bringing me through my desert, and had pitted Himself against my own false idols. And as I hit my flashpoint, as I cried out to God. I watched as He consumed everything with fire—all of my idols, all my false prophets, everything.

So I lay on my bed in the quiet of my room and cried. This was my moment of surrender. I surrendered to the flames the one thing I thought I had control over: my life. It was not time to fear or question the fire, but to step into the blaze and trust I would see the true and living God.

Chapter THIRTEEN

Promises of God

As my mother lay in bed, she heard the world spinning on without her. She listened to the din and chatter of people on the street, the mailman's footsteps on the porch and the creak of the mailbox door. The tick of the sprinkler watering the grass. The shouts of children outside her bedroom window. These sounds reminded her she was alive, but the illness and pain reminded her she was deteriorating. She slept often and was too weak to move much on her own, but whenever she could, she lifted her Bible and read portions of the Psalms.

Her head was bald, exposing a large Frankenstein's monster-like scar and the staples from her second brain surgery. She'd lost her eyebrows and eyelashes because a twenty-four-hour chemotherapy shunt had been placed in her head. It delivered a steady stream of drugs into her body. She lost nearly all mobility in her arms, and she couldn't stand on her own. Her whole body writhed in unrelenting pain. The cancer—and the chemo—attacked her central nervous system, causing her to lose control of her bodily functions. My father bathed her daily because she'd lost her ability to make it to the bathroom on her own.

We knew many people were praying for her. The prayer request for healing had reached faraway places like Japan, random community groups in Wyoming, and of course, our closest friends and family. But with the prayer request came the kinds of stupid things that are often said by well-intentioned people.

When people are in pain or grieving, the last thing they need is a spoonful of religious syrup. I didn't need or want "magnet Christianity" (you know, after the religious sayings that fit perfectly on magnets you hang on your refrigerator). I wanted honest hope. People in pain don't need Band-Aids for their emotional bullet wounds. They need spiritual nurses to instruct them how to keep living in the midst of confusion and pain.

One weekend I walked in on my sickly mother smiling politely and trying her best to sit up straight, even though she was clearly exhausted and in pain. A family friend—a pastor's wife—sat across from her in the living room, speaking incessantly. As I approached, I greeted her guest and propped up pillows to provide comfort to my mother as she lay on the couch. "I was just telling your mom how I lost ten pounds and cycled to Huntington Beach this past weekend. You know, so she can get her mind off of being sick," said her friend.

I felt the blood drain from my face and my chest tighten as I thought to myself, *Is she really talking to my mom about her great body and perfect health, or am I delusional?* I tried to compose myself, but I couldn't completely contain my anger. "Wow, that's great," I said, coolly. "Mom is really tired because she's been given a 30 percent chance to live, so we are praying one day she can walk again. Maybe even cycle to Huntington

Beach." Suddenly aware of her ignorance and my sarcasm, our guest blurted out, "We know all things work for good!," picked up her purse, and left.

After closing the front door behind her (not soon enough for me), I went over to my mother, arms flailing in the air. I was livid! A succession of questions and angry statements about her visitor rolled off my tongue without pause or breath as I went from zero to two hundred in 2.5 nanoseconds.

"How can she call herself your friend? That conversation was a train wreck! Did she really think she was helping? She's so clueless and inconsiderate! I'd rather poke my eyes out with a sharp instrument than hear her talk for one more second."

My mom shushed me and stifled a laugh because not only was I funny, but she also secretly agreed with me. She pulled me close, and I sat on the edge of the couch with my back leaning against her chest. As if she'd read my mind, she opened her dog-eared and highlighted Bible to the book of Psalms. Her frail hands rested on the page as she smiled and read aloud the words of David: "The righteous will flourish like a palm tree, they will grow like a cedar of Lebanon" (Ps. 92:12).

In the left margin of her Bible, she had sketched out a beautiful palm tree and inscribed ***ME*** in black, bold letters beneath her drawing. "Bianca, this doesn't make sense right now, but God spoke to me. In His Word, He spoke to me . . . I'm going to flourish like a palm tree. I'm going to be okay."

UNFAILING LOVE IN DESERT TIMES

My mother's assurance was confusing to me. All signs pointed to deterioration, not just of her body, but of my hope. I wanted to believe her; I wanted to believe she was right; I just couldn't reconcile *how* it would happen.

And I wasn't the only one who was lost. My father continued to lead the church, and my siblings tried continuing on with their lives, but we were all watching a loved one suffer. We wanted the world to stop and grieve with us, but people's everyday lives went on, their doctor appointments, church obligations, college exams, basketball practices. We were lost in the shuffle, struggling to find ways to make it through.

But when we face difficult moments—the loss of a loved one, the pain of a broken dream, or the mourning of a shattered heart—we need to put one foot in front of the other and believe God will lead us to the place we need to be.

But *where* is that place? *What* is that place? As Christians, our hope is that we will make it through the desert wilderness. We can't see the end, but just as God has brought through those who have gone before us, we must believe He is able to do the same for us.

If love is not only what God *does*, but who He *is*, our hope is in Him and the promise of His Word.

He will lead us.

He will guide us.

He will provide for us.

He will refine us.

He will give us what we need in the midst of our confusion.

THE PIT AFTER THE PEAK

Moses and the Israelites sang a song of celebration after God rescued them from the Egyptian army. From lament, He led them into praise. They had witnessed the miraculous—they fled captivity, saw the parting of the Red Sea, and walked across it on dry ground across the sea floor before the waters closed on their Egyptian pursuers, drowning them all. The Israelites could not help but rejoice. With tambourines and a chorus of voices, they sang a song of praise recorded in Exodus. In complete confidence and excitement, they sang out, "In your unfailing love you will lead the people you have redeemed. In your strength you will guide them to your holy dwelling" (Ex. 15:13).

The words they sang strike an ironic contrast to their waning faith and forgetful hearts. The children of Israel needed to hold on to the words they sang, because they were about to hit another bump in the road—or in desert talk, the pit after the peak.

The children of Israel had just finished their desert praise party and dance off, rejoicing because the Egyptians had been defeated, when the story took a twist. After their miraculous escape from captivity, the Israelites faced a new challenge: thirst.

They had gone without water for three days. It was hot, they were wandering, they were following someone they both liked and hated, and now they were dying of thirst. Sound melodramatic? It's not. Medical studies agree that the longest a human can go without water is three days. And there they were, walking and wandering and whispering to each other about how thirsty they were.

They grumbled and complained against Moses, and when they finally found water, it was as bitter as their hearts. They were undone. The hands on the hips, the rolling of the eyes, the sighing and nagging all clearly indicated they were Puerto Ricans—I mean, they were upset.

Yet again, God provided exactly what they needed at just the right time.

In Moses' moment of need, he cried out to the Lord. The Lord answered, showed him a piece of wood, and commanded him to throw it into the water (Ex. 15:25). Once the wood was thrown into the water, it became drinkable. Theologians and horticulturists agree that certain trees can sweeten water and make it drinkable. None of these trees, however, exists in the desert. That piece of wood Moses tossed in the water was a straight-up miracle!

After providing fresh water for them, God led His people to Elim, where they were surrounded by seventy palm trees. It's worth noting here, that the palm is mentioned in the Bible throughout the Old and New Testaments with great significance and meaning. It is used to signify abundance. The palm is the tree of provision.

THE PALM TREE

To my mother and me, the palm tree symbolized a promise. Buried in the Psalms was the hope Mom was going to be okay. And as we lay on the couch, God provided a word, even though it felt like it was too late. When we think we are on the ledge and death waits over the edge, God reveals it's not a ledge but merely a curb. As He can make bitter water sweet, He can makes ledges into curbs; He can make broken lives whole. Our God can bring us to the place of palm trees.

Growing up in California, I saw palm trees everywhere. But the palm tree has great biblical significance and purpose. Palms were prophetically referenced in the Old Testament, they can bear fruit for up to a century, and palm leaves were used to welcome the Messiah into Jerusalem (see John 12:13). It seems to me palm trees are worthy of some attention, no?

During their desert journey, the Israelites found rest and peace in the shade of **seventy** palm trees and an oasis of water in the midst of desolate terrain (Ex. 15:27). What a gift that much-needed place of respite must have been! I found similar solace in the promise of the palm during my own wandering. Mom's verse provided shade in my personal desert and an oasis in my wilderness.

I shifted to the edge of the couch, picked up my mother's Bible, and placed it on my lap. I stared at her drawing next to Psalm 92:12: "The righteous will flourish like a palm tree, they will grow like a cedar of Lebanon."

As my mother read this passage and whispered her belief in full healing, I knew I *needed* to dig in to what this passage signified. If I were to hold on to hope, I knew I would find it in the truth of God's Word. Nothing was going to make more sense in a season of confusion than the simplicity of Psalms.

I went to my father's home office and pulled the first commentary I saw off the bookshelf. The gold lettering on the maroon-colored spine made me feel like I was choosing the most academic research resource. If Psalm 92:12 was my mother's promise, I wanted to make sure I knew what it was about, for whom it was intended, and how we could make this Scripture come to life for my mom.

In Charles Spurgeon's commentary on the passage, I read that palms endure for centuries, unlike any other tree. Spurgeon paralleled the strength and sustainability of a palm in the desert to godly people who stand for righteousness and aim for the glory of God. No matter the circumstance, the godly live and thrive where everything else perishes. Scripture not only tells us what righteous people are, but what they will become. "Come what may, the good man shall flourish, and flourish after the noblest manner."*

As my mom held on to Psalm 92:12, I looked at the significance of the palm tree and began to understand its characteristics and properties. It became a beacon of hope in the darkest of moments, and continues to be an important symbol to me today.

The palm tree is unlike any tree in that it breaks things that try to bind it. While other trees absorb wires or bands, the palm is the only tree that can break any binding around its trunk. As my mom held on to the belief that she was going to flourish like a palm, I held on to the belief that nothing could bind the work of the Lord in her life. Nothing could bind her identity; no wire could pierce her trunk. Very few trees can grow in the desert, but the palm not only grows and flourishes; it produces fruit. The roots of a palm creep deep down into hot sands to find water below the dry surface. Other trees—and people—might become uprooted in desert terrain because there is little capacity to grow strong roots there. But as Jeremiah says, "Blessed is the one who trusts in the Lord,

---

* Spurgeon, Charles R. *Psalms, Volume II (*Wheaton, IL: Crossway, 1993), 33.

whose confidence is in him. They will be like a tree planted by the water that sends out its roots by the stream. It does not fear when heat comes; its leaves are always green. It has no worries in a year of drought and never fails to bear fruit" (Jer. 17:7–8).

Natural disasters wreak havoc on some of the strongest trees, while palm trees remain. No matter what raging winds her life would bring, my mother would stand like a palm. The storms of life would not ravage her roots, roots that were deep and wide. She would bend but not break.

In the midst of Mom's cancer—her desert, if you will—she was an oasis to many people. I remember people constantly telling me how they had approached my mom, wanting to encourage her in her illness, yet left her presence feeling they were the ones who had been encouraged. My mother provided shade and water to weary people.

In Exodus 15, the Israelites were refreshed and rejuvenated as they camped near the streams of water at Elim. A gathering of palm trees is a sure sign of water for the people of God. And my mother, like a single palm or like seventy, would be an oasis for others for as long as God allowed her to live.

BELIEVING GOD

The Israelites, wandering in the wilderness, had seen God do the impossible. And I had witnessed the miraculous things God had done in my own life. But oh, how quickly we forget.

Just as the Israelites forgot how God freed them from Egypt, I had forgotten about the provisions we had been given during my childhood. As the Israelites forgot about how God parted the Red Sea and allowed them to walk across on dry ground, I forgot about traveling in a car our family received as a benevolent gift. As the Israelites forgot how God had delivered manna to feed them daily, I forgot the daily miracles God had done in my life.

When we forget about what God *has* done, it makes us doubt what He *can* do. When we remember His promises, when we remember His goodness, when we remember His miracles, we can hold on to hope that He will rescue us in our time of need.

WHEN WE FORGET ABOUT WHAT GOD *HAS* DONE, IT MAKES US DOUBT WHAT HE *CAN* DO.

Holding my mother's Bible in my hands, I desperately wanted to believe she would be healed. Psalm 92:12 was an oasis for her just as Elim was for the Israelites. She was refreshed and renewed in the shade of God's Word. I looked at my frail mother and saw the peace in her eyes and the faith in heart. Contrary to medical evaluations, she hoped.

She was a living illustration of Romans 4. "Against all hope, Abraham in hope believed . . . Yet he did not waver through unbelief regarding the promise of God, but was strengthened in his faith and gave glory to God, being fully persuaded that God had power to do what he had promised" (Rom. 4:18–21). My mother was a modern-day Abraham. Against all hope, in hope she believed. In spite of the silence of God and the sickness she faced, she believed God would reveal His goodness in her life. She trusted in God's Word for her, that she would rise like a palm tree. And as her roots grew deep in the Word of God, I knew I had to grow roots of my own. I needed to come through my season of fire growing in my faith, my roots stretching deep into the hope of God. This was something my mother couldn't do for me. I had to do it for myself. I had to grow up. I had to grow roots.

Chapter **FOURTEEN**

Community

I had an amazing group of friends (shout out to the Bomb Squad), all of whom I'd known for years. But distance, new jobs, and changing seasons had pulled us all in different directions. The closeness we once enjoyed through proximity suffered, leaving me isolated and afraid of meeting new people. I soon noticed how easy it had become to go to church, sit in the back, and leave without connecting with anyone. I liked being able to mask my issues and disappear when I felt uncomfortable.

Something needed to change; *I* needed to change.

For the first time in years, I forced myself to be honest with where I was in my life. All pride was gone. No veneer was thick enough or high enough to cover the pile of ash that was my life. I no longer had the will to pretend all was well with my soul. Gone was the desire for escape. What I longed for was personal revival. After considering my conversation with Kathy at the women's retreat, I realized the importance of honesty and community; isolation was proving to be dangerous. Whether in trial or triumph, promise or pain, we weren't created to handle life alone.

Everything—the loss of relationships, career advancement, beating back my mother's well-meaning but emotionally unintelligent visitors—was exhausting. I realized that if transformation was to occur and God's presence was to be revealed, I needed to be in relationship with people. Joshua going into battle? He needed community! Jesus changing the world? He did it in community! Paul penning his letters to the early church? He composed in community! Open-fisted, I relinquished control and let new friends into the house I'd built in isolation.

I felt awkward and clumsy. It was worse than a teenage introvert asking a popular kid on a date. But I walked up to two girls I knew marginally—Jeanette and Diane—and nervously asked them if they would be my friends. It was seriously awkward. I didn't think about what would happen if they said no, but thank goodness they didn't. Both said they were looking for people they could be fully honest with in a Christian context. Jeanette was married and a new mom. Diane was single and worked in corporate America. Like opposites, we attracted. We were sensitive to each other's schedules, but intentional in making time to meet.

Over the following months, which rolled into years, we celebrated birthdays and successes, and held each other up through full-on failures. After my flashpoint in the desert, after everything turned to ash, they became my oasis, my palm trees, the answer to my cry. They became living reminders of God's promise that He would give me what I needed if I only bowed in humility and cried out.

Trusting in God, we marched through life together. One foot in front of the other, one day after another, we believed

God was not finished with our lives. His promises were simply yet to be fulfilled. Together we committed to being truthful in the struggle and hopeful in the chaos.

Showing weakness makes you vulnerable, but vulnerability displays your strength. It's a paradox you can understand only when you've survived being honest about where you are in life. I once heard author Brené Brown say, "What makes you vulnerable makes you beautiful."

What do you do when everything has been consumed, when nothing is left? You do things you never thought you would willingly do. With humility and in utter desperation, I confessed to my trusted friends how burdened I felt. I believed God's Word and knew that if we confessed our sins and prayed for each other, we would be healed. (Give me James 5:16 ALL day!) I cried out to God, and I firmly believe He sent me community to stand with me when I felt weak. It wasn't easy. It wasn't natural. It wasn't quick. But it was needed.

So, "community," "doing life," and "fellowshipping with people" are all things I realized I needed. But these can seem like empty Christian buzzwords if we don't explore what they *really* mean. True community means a willingness to take off your mask and let down your facade. But how can we allow ourselves to be vulnerable and transparent when we don't know who we can trust? The answer is simple: find people who are looking for the same thing.

BAND OF BROTHERS

In times of fire, friends are a necessity. I know this firsthand. But beyond my own experience, Scripture teaches us this very same principle. The Bible is chock-full of beautiful stories of friends who stood together even when things got hot.

There's an amazing account in the book of Daniel of three friends who demonstrate the power of unity, solidarity, and faith under fire. Literally.

Daniel chronicles Israel's exile from Judah and the capture of some young Hebrew elites, who were to be trained in the royal palace of the Babylonian king, Nebuchadnezzar. Of Nebuchadnezzar's exiles, four—Daniel, Shadrach, Meshach, and Abednego—stood out above the rest and were elevated to positions of influence and power.

Now imagine they're all at a massive party, a celebration to dedicate a statue commissioned by King Nebuchadnezzar. This wasn't just a ribbon-cutting ceremony at Town Hall with a comically large pair of scissors. It was a major rager, and everyone and their moms were invited! The who's who of the time (AKA the political leaders and officials) joined the ceremony, and as they assembled before this colossal, ninety-foot golden statue, they bowed in unison (Dan. 3).

We don't know what the statue represented, but some people believe it was made in the likeness of King Nebuchadnezzar himself. If it was indeed Nebuchadnezzar, it would be a more ostentatious move than even Kanye West could pull off. As a reference point to help us grasp the size of this statue, the iconic Christ the Redeemer statue in Rio de Janeiro, Brazil, is 125 feet tall, and it's made of stone. Picture a similar statue of solid gold, sparkling in the sun, with thousands of people gathered around to worship. And then consider this: whoever failed to bow down and worship the statue was thrown into a furnace of white-hot fire. (The Babylonians didn't mess around! They were serious about their gods, their worship, and their rules.)

Well, the four Hebrew exiles had gained favor with the king. And of course, when people are elevated, haters arise. We are told a group of tattletales came to King Nebuchadnezzar and accused Shadrach, Meshach, and Abednego of refusing to bow in worship before the idol. This wasn't a lie. The three teens served the one true God and remembered the first command delivered by Moses:

> *I am the* LORD *your God, who brought you out of Egypt, out of the land of slavery. You shall have no other gods before me. You shall not make for yourself an image in the form of anything in heaven above or on the earth beneath or in the waters below. You shall not bow down to them or worship them; for I, the* LORD *your God, am a jealous God . . . (Ex. 20:2–5)*

In community—the three of them together—Shadrach, Meshach, and Abednego remembered. They did not adopt the Babylonian forms of worship or identity. They stayed true, even though it meant the furnace. Shadrach, whose Israelite name meant *beloved by God*; Meshach, whose Israelite name meant *who is as God*; and Abednego, whose Israelite name meant *the Lord is my God*; remained true to their one true God, their desert deliverer.

But would God honor their fidelity?

CHOICES AND OFFERS

Sometimes we want bargains or easy ways out of hard situations. Sometimes we want to be plucked from the desert or the furnace. It's normal. And sometimes, worshiping a false god—even the gods of materialism, relationships, or health—seems like the easy way out. But just because there's an easy road doesn't mean it's the right road.

If I had been around during the time of King Nebuchadnezzar, I fear my desire for safety and oh, I don't know, *living,* would have trumped my convictions. Let's put ourselves in the boys' shoes (well, sandals). They had been trafficked from their homeland. Their parents were most likely dead. They were thrown into a new culture, new language, and new religion—an astrology-based cult we'd consider nothing short of witchcraft. They'd found favor and influence, but they also acquired some haters and dissenters who wanted to destroy them, wanted to set up their demise. Would I be able to withstand such pressures? Would you?

Thousands, if not millions, bowed down to a graven god of gold. Music bumped, the party swung in full effect, everyone came for the festivities—and there were our Hebrew heroes, undoubtedly discussing the situation, possibly praying to the one true God about the choice they were going to have to make.

This narrative that took place thousands of years ago, but aren't we faced with similar decisions today? Do we bow to the little idols that exist in our everyday lives? Do we relinquish our convictions when the social pressure is on? In my desert wilderness, I tried anesthetizing emotions and desires so I didn't have to feel anymore. Chronic shopping? Yes. Credit card debt? Absolutely. Eating to numb the pain? Sure. I suffered from Desert Brain and forgot the ways God had provided for me and my family for so long. I forgot my God-given name: Child of God. Granted, most of us will never encounter a ninety-foot statue of gold we're expected to worship, but there are ways we bend our knee to keep ourselves safe, to go unnoticed, to avoid the fire.

Don't have the money to buy the perfect clothes you want? Charge them to your credit card. Your name is **Not Enough**.

Don't have what they have? Gossip about them until you feel better about yourself. Your name is **Bitter Envy**.

Don't have the perfect marriage to the perfect person? Download some porn. Your name is **Justified Addict**.

Don't like looking at yourself in the mirror? Buy some diet pills or get liposuction. Your name is **Ugly**.

Don't have a way to relax? Have five glasses of wine. Why stop at one? Your name is **All Alone**.

Above any name given to us, by ourselves or others, the name we must never forget is Child of God. As children of the one true God, there is no power, stronghold, or addiction that can overtake us. He is in our past, with us in the present, and orchestrating our future. The moment we forget who we are, we find ourselves bowing down to little gods with no power to transform us.

THROUGH THE FIRE

Shadrach, Meshach, and Abednego were confronted by Nebuchadnezzar, who asked whether it was true—*had they refused to bow to the idol?* They confirmed their disobedience, and in a bold declaration, they informed the king that God would rescue them from the fieriest furnace. But even if He didn't, they said, they would *never* bow down to the image of gold. I don't know how you read your Bible, but these boys just stood up and defiantly punked the king! What confidence. What faith. What gall. But when you know who you are and you know who you serve, you have the boldness to declare God's will above everything. Even living.

Shadrach, Meshach, and Abednego confessed their faith *before entering* the fire, but their faith was proved *in* the fire. It wasn't until their faith was tested that it became real not only to them, but to everyone around them.

Since the boys refused to bow, the king ordered them into the fiery furnace. One by one, they were all cast into the fire. But something amazing happened: instead of dying in the furnace, the witnesses noticed them walking around in the fire. Even more amazingly, King Nebuchadnezzar himself saw a fourth person in the flames. Bible scholars debate who this fourth figure in the fire was, but I believe it was a theophany. **In the fire, the very presence of God was revealed to this band of brothers.**

Our deliverance isn't going to come from *outside* the furnace. The only way to get free is to go *through* the fire. It's in the fire that we are refined. It's in the fire that we are freed. The very thing that is supposed to kill us can free us, helping us enter the presence of God in ways we've never known before.

I know it wasn't until I stood firmly on the promises of God that I was able to withstand my own furnace. And my community of friends? They made it easier. Nothing made sense and nothing seemed safe, but I knew I had to walk into what God was calling me into. It was as if He whispered, *Embrace the unknown and trust that transformation is awaiting you.*

OUR DELIVERANCE ISN'T GOING TO COME FROM *OUTSIDE* THE FURNACE. THE ONLY WAY TO GET FREE IS TO GO *THROUGH* THE FIRE.

The prophecy stated in Isaiah 43 was proven in the lives of these young men. As children they would have been taught to memorize the verses of the prophets—the same verses I memorized in Mr. Charles's Sunday school class. Scripture would have reminded them of their heritage and destiny. They would've read the prophets, like I read the prophets, and perhaps remembered these words:

"When you pass through the waters, I will be with you; and when you pass through the rivers, they will not sweep over you. When you walk through the fire, *you will not be burned*; the flames will *not set you ablaze*" (Isa. 43:2, emphasis mine).

With the support of my friends and my new understanding of how God was using the fire in my life, I surrendered and boldly declared, *God, I know You can heal my mom. But even if You don't, I choose You. I will not bow down to false idols anymore. I will not give up on Mom or You. I am Yours. Have Your way.*

Chapter **FIFTEEN**

Hearing from God

As a church kid, I grew up around a lot of Christians. As a pastor's kid, I knew Bible stories and theology better than I knew American history. As my parents' kid, I saw them hear from God in distinct ways and assumed I would grow up and learn to hear from God the same way. Whether my parents were teaching the Bible or praying for people, it was like they had a direct line to God the way Commissioner Gordon had the red phone to Batman.

But I was an adult (or at least looked like one) and I still didn't "hear from God" the way I thought I was supposed to. My law-loving, self-sufficient, legalistic side did all the right things. From praying *with* people to being prayed over *by* people to reading my Bible and studying exegetically, I wanted to know God's will for my life and hear from Him like I'd been told I could. I knew, as a follower of Christ who was filled with the Spirit, I had the ability to hear from God; I just didn't know how.

Of course, our ultimate guide to knowing God and His will for our lives is the Bible. But after years of reading line upon line, verse upon verse, chapter upon chapter, and book upon book of the Bible, I was discouraged and felt abandoned in my quest to hear from God. If His voice was a radio frequency, I was on a completely different bandwidth.

I thought you were supposed to hear God in a particular way, but as Kathy had reminded me at the retreat, there are many different ways we can hear from Him. In moments when I thought God was silent, He was actually speaking to me, but in ways that were different from what I expected.

Through the prompting of the Holy Spirit, we have direct access to hear from God. We might not hear Him the way other people do, but we need to trust that God is speaking to us, and through us, by His Spirit.

I don't want to oversimplify things, but in studying how to hear from God, I came across some language from my friend Havilah Cunnington that can help identify and equip us to detect the voice of God. Again, I don't want to categorize or limit the nature of God, but for simplicity's sake, I'll break down the four types of human personalities—the knowers, seers, hearers, and feelers—and share how those personalities can learn to hear from God.

Knowers use their intuition or instinct to understand the voice of God. They simply have a "gut" sense, or they intrinsically know something. Whether it's an impression or mental conviction, knowers have an ability to push through barriers and are commonly right about the ways things will turn out. When they encounter the word of God, little will stop their conviction and resolve.

One biblical example of a knower comes from the book of Joshua. In chapter 7, verses 10–11, we read that Joshua knew about Achan's sin and the items he stole during a raid.

Another example of a knower is illustrated in 2 Kings, the time Elisha knew through revelation that Gehazi had lied to Naaman for his own gain (2 Kings 5:20–27).

Acts 16 provides another example of a knower. Paul, who had seen visions and physically heard from God, simply decided intuitively to bring Timothy on his journey with him. We see the fruit of his *knowing* by the church and ministry that was the result of Timothy's life.

Seers know how things should be because of the visual images they receive. Once they get a vision from God, they are filled with faith and believe it's not a matter of *if* but *when* the vision will come to pass.

When God speaks to seers, they see something either with their natural eyes or, more commonly, in their spirit. A vision can be a stationary picture, moving images, or a dream in sleep.

We have a biblical accounts of two prophets who were seers. In 1 Chronicles, the Bible records the events of King David's reign and says, "from beginning to end, they are written in the records of Samuel the **seer**, the records of Nathan the prophet and the records of Gad the **seer**" (1 Chron. 29).

Hearers hear the voice of God. Whether it's an audible sound or a voice from within, hearers can discern what God is saying. They have strong convictions that what they hear is the truth and hold on to the word the Lord has spoken to them. Because they can specifically pinpoint a time or place God spoke to them, their confidence is grounded in what they heard from God.

In 1 Samuel 3, the young prophet Samuel heard from God directly. Whether it was an audible voice or something Samuel heard within, it is a beautiful example of God speaking to one of His children directly. Samuel answered faithfully, "Speak, Lord. Your servant is listening." In Acts 9, God also spoke directly to Paul. We know it was audible because the men who traveled with Paul heard it too (Acts 9:7).

And finally, there are **feelers**—my favorites. Feelers are used to being interrupted by God emotionally, and have insights to the emotions of God in unprecedented ways. Feelers tend to be able to pick up on the feelings of others or be able to "feel" an environment. Because they are prone to sensing emotion and atmosphere, they can catch spiritual moments others might miss.

During Pentecost, the Holy Spirit came mightily and changed many lives. The New King James Version describes a fear that came over people's souls, and the New International Version says they were filled with awe (Acts 2:43a). Their feelings preceded the signs and wonders that followed (Acts 2:43b).

God can reveal Himself through His Word (information) and through the prophetic (revelation). Both are needed for balance, and together they allow us to experience God in ways we never thought possible. When we understand the different ways God brings us His revelations, we can be bold and believe that God *is* speaking to us.

LISTEN

I sat in an auditorium filled with almost a thousand youth pastors and youth volunteers. Worship music played in the background, yet there was a stillness. Church staff and volunteers from around the nation were gathered for an annual youth workers' conference. We were told there would be a night of worship, where we'd be encouraged to pray for our youth ministries, churches, and co-laborers. I was attending the conference alone and didn't know many people. But the organizer of the conference was a longtime friend and had encouraged me to attend, even if I came solo.

On the last night Britt Merrick, my friend (and the organizer of the conference), spoke about how he wanted us to hear from God, to trust God to move in our hearts and lives. Although I had been a Christian for a long time, I felt like a toddler just learning how to walk and talk. My newfound faith—the one born of desert fire—may have been wobbly, but I was taking steps toward trusting God daily. I'd shed the rote religious repertoire of my veneered faith, stretched it into simpler, child-like language. *Dear God, I know You're there, so like, um—can You talk to me?* Clearly my prayer life was both prolific and profound. I stared at a verse I had written on the inside cover of my Bible, *Be still and know*, and believed it was *my* verse. As clearly as God spoke to Mr. Charles and my mom and Kathy, He could, I believed, speak to me too. I wanted—no, I *needed*—to hear from God. And I knew I had to be still.

During our time of worship, I sat down for a moment and closed my eyes to pray. *Dear God, I want to—uh, like, really experience You. I mean, I know You're there and I know You love me, but speak to me. I know You can.* As I settled into this prayer, I saw the word *sex* appear. I immediately opened my eyes and thought, *What the heck am I thinking about?! I'm in church!* (To be totally clear, I didn't envision people having sex, but simply saw the three letters appear in my mind. And let's be real:

as a twenty-seven-year-old virgin, I probably couldn't have pictured the act anyway.)

I immediately began shaming myself for not focusing on our time of worship. But I remembered Kathy in her white orthopedic shoes a year earlier at the women's retreat reminding me to test things in Scripture and pray through all things. *God will reveal and bring clarity when He is speaking to you,* she'd said.

My heart pounded in my chest. Was this from God? Was He speaking to me? WHY DID THIS HAVE TO BE ABOUT SEX?

I sat in my chair, worship music filling the room around me, and I didn't know what to do. Like the doubting warrior Gideon in the Old Testament, I made excuses and told God He had to confirm to me what in the world was going on. I prayed this faith-filled prayer: *God, if You are telling me something, prove it.* Being the word nerd I am, I did the only thing I knew to do: I grabbed my Bible. I would never suggest doing this, because hearing from God isn't like roulette where you randomly get a number or a word from Him. I was, however, desperate and naive. I prayed, *God, if this is You speaking to me, show me through Your Word.* I thumbed through the middle of the Bible and opened a random page, testing the prompting of God like Gideon.

The first verse my eyes fell on was Job 31:1: "I made a covenant with my eyes not to look lustfully at a young woman." My eyes widened, and I slammed my Bible shut. The beat of my heart quickened, and it was like I instantly knew what was going on. God revealed something to me in a divine manner. I heard God. I knew I heard Him, but I didn't know what to do.

As this was going on, Britt approached the microphone and announced, "Jesus said we have an advocate and encourager in His Holy Spirit to speak and bring things to light. I believe God is speaking to some of you here even now, through words of knowledge, or words of encouragement, or words of prophecy." I was familiar with the passages in Romans and 1 Corinthians about the gifts of the Holy Spirit, but this was only the second time I had been in an environment where we were invited to participate in exercising these gifts openly and with such calm control.

I slumped in my chair and tried to avoid Britt's line of sight, afraid he might be talking to me. How could he know I'd just heard from God? And what was I supposed to do with my knowledge?

Britt gave an open invitation toward the microphone and welcomed people to the stage to share Scriptures, words of encouragement, or anything else stirring in their hearts. Then he returned to his seat. No one moved as the band continued playing. I can't explain what happened inside me with any word but *compelled*. I was compelled to stand up, walk through the crowded auditorium, and tell Britt what I believed God had shown me.

Trying to be discreet, I walked around the periphery of the auditorium. As people went on singing, I approached Britt. I squatted in front of him and motioned for him to come close so I could whisper to him. He leaned in, and I said, "Someone in here is sleeping with someone they aren't married to, and God is calling them out. K, bye."

He reached for my shoulder to keep me from rushing away and said boldly, "Go share it."

The blood drained from my face and my heart beat so hard I felt blood pulsing in my temples. I told Britt no. He told me yes. I said I couldn't. He said I could. He won.

He stood up and put his arm around my shoulder to usher me onstage. Worship quieted for a moment as he explained to the listening crowd that I was going to share something. As I approached the podium, I exhaled, closed my eyes for a second, and then boldly repeated what I had told Britt moments earlier.

A word of knowledge is a definite conviction or knowledge that comes through a particular Scripture, vision, or dream. It is supernatural insight or understanding of circumstances, situations, problems, or facts by *revelation* (which is a fancy word that explains knowing something through divine help, not human wisdom).

The word I heard was clear, I knew in my heart beyond the shadow of a doubt that God had spoken to me, and I knew what He was saying. The band stopped playing as I said, "There is a youth pastor in here who is sleeping with one of his volunteers. You know this is wrong, but you have not stopped. Very clearly, you are to bow out of ministry and repent, or you will take your whole youth ministry down with you."

The moment I stepped offstage, my hands began to tremble. I was literally shaking with fear. I suddenly felt like everything I had just said was made up. The confidence I had, just moments earlier, melted away as I returned to my seat. Never had I felt more stupid than in that moment as shame began to creep in, filling my mind. *God didn't speak to you. You just made that up. Do you really need* so *much attention that you made up a lie?*

The night ended in prayer, and I quietly exited the building before everyone was dismissed. I wanted to get to my room before I had to make eye contact with anyone. In the fashion of an Olympic speed walker, I raced out of the building. I had almost reached the dorm where I was staying when I was stopped by one of the conference coordinators.

Out of breath from chasing me from the auditorium, he told me he wanted to confirm the word I'd spoken. My eyes widened, and my jaw dropped open in shock. He went on to explain that he couldn't share details out of respect for those involved, but a youth pastor had come forward for prayer and confessed that he was having an affair with one of his volunteers, a volunteer who was actually with him at the conference. Both confessed their sin tearfully and repentantly, and said they knew they had to remove themselves from ministry.

What I wanted to do: Bust out a praise hanky, jump up and down, and throw my arms around his neck in sheer excitement that (1) I wasn't a false prophet (which, in OT times, could've gotten me stoned for heresy), and (2) I'd heard from God and I wasn't crazy.

What I did: Thanked him casually like a sane person would do and told him how grateful I was that he filled me in and confirmed what God had told me.

Back in my dorm room, before any of my roommates arrived, I called my mom. In utter excitement I recounted the entire story for her again and again until she had no more questions. We both giggled with delight and praised God not only for bringing restoration and freedom for the two leaders involved in the affair, but for the promise of God to speak to His children (John 14:16–17).

I lay in bed that evening and thanked God. It wasn't a rote activity. I repeated the words of one of my favorite authors, "Please God, please God, please God," and "Thank You, thank You, thank You." His presence was so near, His words were so real, His promises were fulfilled. I closed my eyes and felt like the words of Samuel (1 Sam. 3:10) had come true for me. The songs I had sung in the desert had made their way to the ears of God. For the first time in three years my heart was certain God heard my deepest cry: *Speak, Lord, I'm listening.*

WANDERINGS IN THE WILDERNESS

Though desert seasons seem never-ending, we know all things eventually do come to an end. The book of Deuteronomy chronicles the latter part of the Israelites' exodus journey. After forty years of wandering, God spoke to Moses, and something changed.

In the beginning of the second chapter of Deuteronomy, there's a chapter heading in big, bold black letters. (Well, you'll have that heading if you have a fancy Bible with maps in the back and a concordance. If you don't have one, ask your pastor to give you one. Pastors will *always* give you a good Bible. I'm pretty sure it's in their job description.) Anyway, the section heading is straightforward: *Wandering in the Wilderness.* This is the first time language actually explains that the previous forty years were simply wanderings. And it's here that things began to shift.

It was probably an average day in the desert, like the day before, and the day before, and the day before the day before.

The children of Israel were wandering. One foot in front of the other, day after day, week after week, month after month, for forty years. But on this particular day, something changed. God spoke to Moses, saying, "You have made your way around this hill country long enough; now turn north" (Deut. 2:3).

Isn't that how life works sometimes? We pray, beat our chests, cry, scream, kick, and then, without fanfare or dramatics, the Lord responds. When we reach the end of ourselves, when we surrender, He speaks, and life changes. This is the way it was with the Israelites. All those years, they called out to God. All those years, I prayed for something to change too. But God didn't respond at first. Sometimes, His response only comes after transformation.

I thought I wanted a husband and a house on the beach and a mom who didn't have cancer. I thought I wanted status and education and the perfect career. I thought I needed control and perfection and prestige. But in my wilderness wanderings, I discovered all these things were temporal, combustible. The only thing that could meet my deepest need was closeness and communication with God. Hearing from Him brought me complete satisfaction.

Mom still had cancer. I still lived with my parents. My dating record was still pitiful. Nothing had changed—not my circumstances, anyway. But somehow, my spiritual reality had shifted. Even though I was still in the midst of chaos, I experienced the greatest freedom and transformation because I knew God was with me.

I knew things were changing. I believed my Promised Land was near.

Chapter **SIXTEEN**

Empowered

When I was growing up, I believed God promises us fulfillment through the presence of His Spirit, but for so long, it felt like that promise was really for only certain people. The Holy Spirit was reserved for those who didn't watch reality television, sat in the front row at church, or attended charismatic or "Spirit-led" churches. But the more I read and researched the Holy Spirit, the more I discovered the empowerment of the Holy Spirit was for every believer. Even me.

Consider this passage in Luke:

> So I say to you: Ask and it will be given to you; seek and you will find; knock and the door will be opened to you. For everyone who asks receives; the one who seeks finds; and to the one who knocks, the door will be opened. "Which of you fathers, if your son asks for a fish, will give him a snake instead? Or if he asks for an egg, will give him a scorpion? If you then, though you are evil, know how to give good gifts to your children, how much more will your Father in heaven give the *Holy Spirit* to those who ask him!" (Luke 11:9–13, emphasis mine)

The Holy Spirit is promised to those who ask. So I did, just like that. Not just for a crutch or as a coping mechanism, I asked for *all* the fruit of the Holy Spirit and *all* His gifts. I literally prayed for a double dose of the Holy Ghost! If Jesus said to ask for the Spirit and He will be given to you, then I was going to take Him at His word. Whether God was going to heal my mom, I realized, wasn't the point. For the first time in my life, I wanted the *presence* of God more than I wanted the *power* of God.

HOLY SPIRIT

If we look at the scope of what Jesus did here on earth, His works are both natural—loving the outcasts, talking to the unclean, and forgiving enemies—and supernatural—healing the lame, causing the blind to see, bringing the dead to life. But before He left this earth, Jesus promised His disciples that they would do greater works than He did through the power of the Holy Spirit.

When we talk about the Holy Spirit, we might have different reactions. If you grew up in a charismatic environment, this might inspire you to grab your tambourine, pick up your praise banner, and run around in a church sanctuary. If you grew up in a more conservative environment (like I did), you might want to hide because the idea of speaking in tongues and talking about the "Holy Ghost" is just plain scary. All my life I credited the Holy Spirit with things that seemed to be supernatural, while dismissing or overlooking His presence in daily, natural things. Unless crazy things happened—mysterious checks given to us to cover our rent, miraculous food arriving in times of need—I didn't recognize the Holy Spirit at work in the everyday.

In the documented life of Jesus, we see His everyday actions, from playing with children to discussing theology, as examples of how we are to live. Jesus' demeanor was centered on love, grace, and kindness. Do we need the Holy Spirit for this? Absolutely! (If you ever have to manage screaming children, you will definitely need the power of God to survive.)

Jesus also did some pretty gnarly things we would classify as supernatural. He prophetically spoke over people, multiplied meals, and had the ability to control weather patterns (Sea of Galilee, anyone?). Jesus' daily life was imbued with the power of the Spirit.

For the first time in my life, at the women's retreat with my mom, surrounded by women of great faith, I had a tangible, real-life experience of the fullness of the Spirit, the ultimate promise of God. I witnessed the reconciliation of relationships, the restoration of hope, and the powerful proclamation of God's Word. But I also witnessed the supernatural power of an extraordinary God moving in the lives of ordinary people—power that cannot be explained except by way of the Holy Spirit. It took me some time before I felt the Spirit move that way again, but that retreat was the beginning.

Looking back on all the supernatural things I saw and heard that evening, the most miraculous of all was watching women accept Jesus as their personal Lord and Savior. I knew women who had been praying for loved ones—friends, daughters, sisters—and had invited them to the retreat. I watched as these women who were spiritually lost found their way to

Jesus. And that? That was the most beautiful and powerful miracle of all.

And now, I'd had my own Holy Spirit empowerment. I'd seen God speak miraculously from my own mouth at the youth conference. He said we would do greater works than He did, and I believed we coul. Lives were changed and healing occurred through the Father, Son, and Holy Spirit. The very essence of what Christ did on earth—physical and spiritual healing—was happening as we, His people, had the faith to believe in the promises of the constant and faithful One. Could this be the *greater* Jesus promised?

HOLD ON TO THE PROMISE

Before Christ went to the cross, He told His closest friends that if they believed in Him, they would continue to do the works He'd been doing, and in fact, they would do greater things than He'd done (John 14:12). Yes, He was leaving them, but not as orphans. An advocate was coming, He said, one that would be with them forever, which is the Spirit of truth (John 14:16). The advocate—the Holy Spirit—would not only be an advocate, but one to empower their work.

We can brush over these Scriptures without realizing their full implications, but if we pause and think about the amazing gift Jesus gave us, that we are empowered to do *greater* works than He did on this earth, shouldn't this make us tremble? It seems too crazy, too impossible to believe. The God of heaven and earth sent His only Son to live a sinless human life, then take the weight of the world's sins upon Himself, die a horrific death on the cross, and rise from the dead three days later, thereby granting us forgiveness of our sins and the promise of new life. THAT God is inviting us to do greater things in His name, for His glory. Are you kidding me? I tremble just thinking about it.

One of the most poignant scenes in the life of Christ occurs in the garden of Gethsemane. We see the fullness of Jesus' humanity as He cries out to His Father and asks if there is a different way, a way to save the world without sacrificing His life on the cross. He calls out to His Father not once, not twice, but three times.

"Going a little farther, He fell with his face to the ground and prayed, 'My Father, if it is possible, may this cup be taken from me. Yet not as I will, but as you will'" (Matt. 26:39). Jesus longed to be heard by His Father. He cried out to God, but Scripture doesn't say God responded. We can assume since Jesus asked three times, silence was the only thing He heard.

Kneeling on the ground, face pressed into the dirt, He prayed. In moments of crisis or pressure, is our natural reaction to fall to our knees in prayer? My natural reaction is to run away from the fiery furnaces, to try to speed through the deserts. I fill the silence with noise. But the greatest lesson in this scene is Christ's willingness to endure what is to come if it is the will of His Father. Even in the silence.

At His sentencing and crucifixion, Jesus was bruised, beaten, and bloodied; tortured, tormented, and tied to a whipping post. Our Savior endured the most horrific physical pain, but said nothing during His abuse. Then, as He hung on the cross, He uttered the most painful words. But they did not express the agony of His torture; rather, they expressed the pain of being separated from His Father. "My God, my God, why have you forsaken me?" He cried (Matt. 27:46). Like the Israelites in the desert, Jesus cried out to God, even with His last breaths, lamenting the silence and separation from the one He most wanted to be near.

In our moments of pain and confusion, silence and isolation, we must hold on to the promises of God's Word.

What is empty can be filled.

What is broken can be mended.

What is divided can be multiplied.

What is dead can live again.

Jesus Christ is the living proof.

Just as God was faithful to resurrect the Messiah, His Son Jesus Christ, God is faithful to keep His promises to us too. The power that raised Jesus from the grave is alive in us today (Rom. 8:11). And the Spirit is not just promised to perfect people, or pretty people, or polished people, but for all who call on the name of Jesus Christ (Acts 2:21).

WHAT IS EMPTY CAN BE FILLED.
WHAT IS BROKEN CAN BE MENDED.
WHAT IS DIVIDED CAN BE MULTIPLIED.
WHAT IS DEAD CAN LIVE AGAIN.
JESUS CHRIST IS THE LIVING PROOF.

One night after work, while driving home to my parents' house, I found myself in yet another pity party. I was comparing and contrasting my life to everyone else's (yes, *again)*. But right in the middle of that world's best pity party, I stopped myself. I knew I was going down a dangerous road, and I didn't want to wallow in gripe or grief.

With my whole being fighting the words, I uttered a prayer like Jesus' prayer at Gethsemane: *Not my will, but Your will be done.* My eyes clouded with tears, but my thoughts were lucid. I was learning how to surrender my own will to the will of the Father. The last days of Jesus' life demonstrate the beauty of the transformation that occurs when we submit to the will of God.

> He **cried** out to God (Mark 14:35).
>
> He **surrendered** His will (Matt. 26:42).
>
> He **believed** the promise that His death would bring us life (Ps. 22).
>
> He **asked** community to be with Him in the midst of trial (Matt. 26:46).
>
> He **submitted** to God's will even on the cross (Mark 15:34).
>
> He **rose** from the dead (Mark 16:6).

I asked the Holy Spirit to have full reign in my life. I believed the power that resurrected Jesus Christ from the grip of death was alive in me. If Jesus promised me this same transformational power, I wanted it. I wanted *all* of it.

FIREPOWER

About a year after that first women's retreat with Mom, I was invited to teach a Bible study to a group of women at church. I was a bit intimidated because most of the women were older than me, but my mom encouraged me to speak from the heart. The portion of Scripture I was to teach from was—wait for it—Psalm 46:10, "Be still and know that I am God."

I taught that Bible study years ago, but I can still remember how I studied, how I prepared, and how I taught that portion of Scripture. Even today, it's one of my favorite verses because it was so real to me in that season. When the psalmist wrote about lands that shook, waters that overtook, and oceans that roared and foamed, I felt like I intimately knew what he meant. But we are not without encouragement because the writer reminds us that our God is a refuge and strength, our help in times of trouble.

Following the teaching, I welcomed the worship team to lead us in a time of prayer. After calling the prayer team forward, I sat down and started praying for all the women who were coming forward for prayer. As I did, it struck me: *I'm praying for the women and over the women, but I'm afraid to pray with the women.* Deep down somewhere, I still believed my prayers were impotent or less holy than those of the women on the prayer team. (No, but fo'real, those prayer ladies are LEGIT!) I felt like I remained at a safe distance, instead of up close and personal with pain and trauma and need.

As the line of women continued to build, I stood up and walked to the front of the auditorium, whispering a desperate prayer to God, a new kind of cry–not *Hear me*, but *Help me*. The moment I took my place at the front, a woman was already in front of me, eager for prayer. Her large brown eyes filled with tears as she explained that she was infertile and tired of trying every avenue to conceive but still ending up empty. I grabbed her hands and told her I didn't know her pain, but God did. I pulled her close and began to pray over her, for her, and with her. During the prayer I was reminded of Hannah, a barren woman in the Old Testament who begged God for a child. I believed God was speaking to me because my heart's desire was to bless the woman before me in the same way Eli the priest spoke words of blessing and faith over Hannah. I asked if I could place my hand on her abdomen, and when she agreed, I prayed with boldness and belief that she would conceive.

There were no fireworks. No one fell on the floor. There was no glitter falling from heaven. There was only this: a simple prayer. As she walked away, I prayed that what I spoke over her was from Him and not from me.

The Bible study ended, and many months passed. I looked for the woman at church week after week. I wanted to know how she was, but our paths never crossed. Then one day, a year later, someone approached me. I immediately recognized her large brown eyes. The same eyes I'd looked into a year before, eyes filled with tears of sorrow, were now filling with tears of a different kind. I excitedly wrapped my arms around her as she explained that she and her husband had moved away, but they made the trek back to Los Angeles to come to church for the weekend.

Her tears fell heavily as she grabbed my hands and placed them on her abdomen. Her eyes looked directly into mine as she said, "I'm pregnant, Bianca! I'm pregnant!" My hands dropped from her belly in shock. I felt the blood drain from my face. "I'm sorry," I said, confused. "You're what?"

She laughed at my reaction, and through her tears of joy, she explained that the night I prayed over her, she knew something had changed. When I laid my hands on her abdomen, she said she felt the power of God touch her, and a warmth filled her body. As she recounted this, I tilted my head, skeptically squinted my eyes, and tightened my lips.

What the left side of my brain was thinking: THIS IS CRAZY TALK, BRO! I have no idea what you're talking about. I felt nothing. There was nothing. You're trippin', bro. (Side note: I say *bro* when I'm going into shock.)

What the right side of my brain was thinking: I believe in God. I believe in miracles. I believe prayer changes things. This is God. This is a miracle. This is an answer to prayer through the work of the Holy Spirit.

She grabbed my hands again, looked me squarely in the face, and said, "A year ago you told me I was like Hannah and God would give me a child. He did. I have read the story over and over, and Hannah found Eli to tell him her prayers were answered. We drove back to church today to tell you our prayers were answered and that you were part of my miracle."

She pulled out her Bible, opened to the end of Hannah's story, and read the passage out loud.

> "'Sir, do you remember me?' Hannah asked. 'I am the very woman who stood here several years ago praying to the Lord. I asked the Lord to give me this boy, and he has granted my request. Now I am giving him to the Lord, and he will belong to the Lord his whole life.' And they worshiped the Lord there" (1 Sam. 1:26–28 NLT).

As she spoke to me, our eyes locked. "Bianca, you were part of my healing, and now we have to thank God."

I drove home that night in complete awe of who God chooses to use and how. He'd chosen to use me, a daughter who'd just barely made it out of the desert, who'd only just survived the crucible fires. No longer was I a spectator; I was a participant in God's plan.

God speaks to and wants to use all those to call upon His name, even the stragglers who've barely made it out of the desert alive, even those whose lives seem burned to the ground. All it takes is the desperation to cry out in the wilderness, the willingness to walk into the furnace, and faith the size of a mustard seed (Matt. 17:20).

From questioning to believing, from legalism to liberty, from self-sufficiency to supernatural sufficiency, I was being refined in every way possible. And I liked it.

Chapter **SEVENTEEN**

Refined

When I was ten years old, my mother took my siblings and me on a field trip to pan for gold. (Please don't judge us. We were weird.) A kooky mountain guide who wore canvas shorts, wool socks, and hiking boots explained to us the art of gold-mining. He lifted up a massive piece of ore and said that hidden inside was something precious and valuable, but it was going to take patience to get it.

When you're a poor kid and someone tells you there's a possibility of possessing something lucrative, you listen! The hustler inside of me sized up the other kids in our tour and did some mental calculations factoring in drive, tenacity, and stamina. I could outlast them all in the hunt for gold. In my mind, I was going to be *rich* by the time I left for home.

But reality set in when our guide explained that the final step in acquiring gold was to break down the ore, to melt down the various rocks and fire up the gold until the dross—otherwise known as junk—comes to the surface. The fire had to be white-hot, and took continual stoking. We let out a combined sigh of relief because we knew it was way too much work for us kids, and we didn't have the time to wait through the process. We weren't going to be taking any loot home after all.

Without missing a beat, our guide told us that was exactly the reaction most people had when they learned how the process worked, and only dedicated and persevering people obtained the precious metal. "What survives in the fire," he said, "will determine what is truly valuable and real."

As we baked in the sun and scoured rocks, looking for gold-flecked fragments, we patiently tossed aside dirt clogs, stones, and ore. We looked for precious metal amidst common elements. In hindsight, I see it. I might not have struck it rich that day, but I walked away with wisdom more valuable than gold. *What survives in the fire will determine what is truly valuable and real.*

REFINING FIRE

Ore is common, but gold is precious. In life, trials are common, but the faith that carries us through those trials is precious. As laborious as it is to mine gold, developing and refining our faith is equally demanding.

The first chapter of James says we should count it all joy when we face trials because the testing of our faith produces perseverance (vv. 2–3). James isn't saying we should be happy that we have to endure trials; he's saying to mine the joy from the trials, because trials produce in us a quality that a life of ease and comfort won't: the ability to persevere. What's more, and this is just my own two cents, we can *count it all joy* that we serve a God who provides for us in our desert trials, who communes with us and delivers us from our fiery furnace moments. Consider Shadrach, Meshach, and Abednego: they professed their faith *before* entering the fire, but their faith was proven and refined *inside* it.

In the days of waiting for my mother to either beat cancer or not, I'd question when the insanity would stop; I'd cringe when someone slapped a Scripture on the situation like a Band-Aid over a bullet wound and expected the emotional bleeding to stop.

But as much as I wanted to fight against a biblical prescription or a Jesus-y fix, I came across some verses that dressed my wounds and wrapped them in hope, not hype. They came from the first book of Peter, in which the author wrote, "I know how great this makes you feel, even though you have to put up with every kind of aggravation in the meantime. Pure gold put in the fire comes out of it *proved* pure; genuine faith put through this suffering comes out *proved* genuine. When Jesus wraps this all up, it's your faith, not your gold that God will have on display as evidence of his victory" (1 Peter 1:6–7 MSG).

In the days of my fresh faith, I considered that kooky mountain guide from my childhood. He told us that to start, stir up, and heighten a fire hot enough to burn off the dross, oxygen must be present. And if you've ever started a beach bonfire or lit a fire in a rock-ring at a campground, you understand this principle. You've probably fanned a flame to make it grow or blown on smoldering embers to help them ignite. As I walked into new belief, real belief, I felt the winds of change stoking my own faith fire. And these words continued to give me strength to press into the furnace: *what survives in the fire will determine what is truly valuable and real.*

WINDS OF CHANGE

Whipping and snapping violently, the wind beat on the windows as if it was trying to get our attention. Within the safety of the car, we listened to the hiss and wheeze of the storm outside, watched the leaves and trees dance like marionettes controlled by a heavenly puppeteer. We sat in the car in silence, waiting while my dad stood in line to purchase my mother's medications.

Another round of chemo. Another round of cancer. Another round of fighting a capricious and ruinous disease. As the wind blew outside, I felt like I was watching what was going on inside my mother's body. There was movement everywhere. Outside the safety of our car, things thrashed about. Where did the wind come from? Where was it going? Where did the cancer come from? When was it going to end?

We had left the oncology ward of St. Jude's Hospital in a daze. The doctors were unclear about what was going on. They'd labeled my mother a medical anomaly, an undefined case with no direct solution or care. *More chemo*, they said. *More radiation*, they said. *More pain killers*, they said. More, more, more. At what point, I wondered, did *more* become *not enough*?

When you are at the end of yourself, that's when God begins. Maybe that sounds cliché, but it's true. We all—my whole family—were at the end of ourselves, but we believed God was going to do something. He was going to change something. God was going to stoke and fan into flames a fire of faith.

Have you ever wondered how wind is created? Where

does it come from, and where does it go? Although we can feel the wind's presence, we can't see it. Science explains that the air around our globe is in constant motion, and wind is created by changes in pressure and temperature. And as scientifically interesting as that is, I'm more fascinated with how God uses wind throughout Scripture. He's always kicking it up at the most interesting times. Science says changes in pressure and temperature create wind, but doesn't God use wind to bring spiritual change as well?

Take, for example, Moses in Egypt. He was commissioned by God to free the Israelites from Pharaoh and lead them to their Promised Land. Moses knew he was going up against a powerful man, but he trusted God to do the impossible. One of the amazing acts Moses performed by God's power involved wind, a way to usher change in and out and move things around.

Before the children of Israel made it to the Promised Land, before they wandered in the desert wilderness, before they walked on dry ground through the Red Sea, they were in Egypt. After years of captivity and slavery, Moses went to Pharaoh to request freedom for his people. When freedom was denied, Moses warned Pharaoh of the plagues to come.

Exodus 10 records how Moses demanded that Pharaoh let the Israelites go. "'If you refuse to let them go,' he said, '[the Lord] will bring locusts into your country tomorrow'" (v. 4). Pharaoh refused, and Moses stretched his staff over the land of Egypt and brought in an east wind that lasted all day and night, just as the Lord had told him to do. When morning arrived, true to Moses' word and God's promise, locusts filled the land as far as the eye could see. The locusts were the plague, but the wind was what brought the voracious insects into the land.

Like Moses, aren't we carriers of the word of God? Don't we know He will act on our behalf? Like Moses, can't we walk in those promises and believe God is going to move?

When the winds of change came into my life, I had to believe they brought a promise. I had to believe He'd brought me through the desert, out of the furnace, for a purpose.

All around me God was moving and allowing me to pray and participate in His miraculous works. Whether praying for barren wombs or speaking prophetic promises over others, I was desperate for the presence of God. At the same time, I wrestled with the fact that no matter how I prayed, God hadn't healed Mom. I witnessed the healing of people around me while my mother continued to suffer. But surely, I would see God's work again—wouldn't I?

I HAD TO BELIEVE HE'D BROUGHT ME THROUGH THE DESERT, OUT OF THE FURNACE, FOR A PURPOSE.

I looked to Moses on his desert journey, hoping to understand how to move in the midst of these winds. God told him the winds would usher in one of the plagues, and Moses had a choice to either respond or resign. As the story of Moses shows us, when we take God at His word, He sends us what we need so that we might accomplish what He's called us to do.

With every plague that spread over the Egyptian landscape, Moses watched God keep His promises and do the miraculous. Not only does God start things, but He also completes them. When we trust God, He gives us what we need when we need it. And in the case of the Israelites, not only did God usher in the wind to bring the locusts, but He also brought in a wind to push them out. As the book of Exodus tells us, "And the Lord changed the wind to a very strong west wind, which caught up the locusts and carried them into the Red Sea. Not one locust was left anywhere in Egypt" (Ex. 10:19).

This pattern is repeated through the Israelites' journey again and again. In every situation that arose in the desert, Moses followed the same cycle—listen, obey, trust. Just like Moses, I had a choice: I could believe in God's promises and move forward or forget them and quit. I refused to quit. After making it through those barren, silent days, I chose to do what God asked of me because I refused to quit. I needed His presence more than anything.

I had to trust the refiner's fire. Wash, rinse, repeat.

The wind blew into the car as my dad opened the door and quickly got in with the white paper bag containing rattling bottles of medication. He handed the bag to me and said, "Who knew I would be a drug dealer today?" I smiled as I looked at him, this man who had the amazing ability to find humor in the midst of chaos.

My mom, reclining in the passenger seat with her eyes closed, smiled and laughed. Her body was weak; she had lost her appetite for a couple of days thanks to the nauseating effects of the chemotherapy dripping through the shunt embedded in the top of her head. It had been five days since her last infusion, and she looked feeble.

Then, as the wind shook the trees outside our car, my mother suddenly said, "I feel hungry. I want Mexican food."

My father looked at me in excitement and surprise and said, "Let's get tacos and the spiciest salsa we can find!" We sped to the first Mexican restaurant we saw and sat in the Spanish-style courtyard beneath a mural-painted wall—my father, my mother, and me.

The wind continued to blow, and my mother closed her eyes and tilted her face toward the sun. Over chips, guacamole, and tacos, I could see her gaining strength, and with her strength came hope. My dad and I shared glances as we discussed the plans going forward. We held on to God's promise—His ways and thoughts are better than ours (Isa. 55:8–9). We believed God loved Mom and wanted her whole and healthy whether on earth or in heaven. And like Moses, we trusted that God was able to do what He promised to do. We would listen, obey, trust.

God opened nature's storerooms and let the wind stoke His refining fire. Things were changing; I felt it in the wind.

Chapter **EIGHTEEN**

Made New

On a day similar to the one when I received the call from my dad about Mom's cancer, I was working alone when my cell phone rang. This time Dad's voice was calm and calculated, but I could hear the urgency beneath. "B, are you busy?" he asked. "I have something to tell you." I stepped away from my desk and told him I could talk, but suddenly I couldn't breathe. My lungs stopped their expanding and contracting; I closed my eyes and waited for the news.

After three years of doctor visits, surgeries, medical diagnoses and prognoses, we'd come to the end of experimental chemotherapy, alternative options, and medical procedures. If the medicine pumped through Mom's cranial shunt didn't work, there were no options left. That was that.

In the moment before my father spoke, I pictured Mom's shaved head, the surgical scar, the Frankenstein's monster stitches. Every week she drove to the oncology ward at St. Jude's Hospital, and the doctors filled her up with chemicals like she was a car's gas tank being topped off. Except instead of giving her the ability to move forward, the chemo gave her nausea. And fatigue. And migraines. And hair loss. And hydrocephalus. And Bell's palsy.

After three years of medical misdiagnoses, two years of battling cancer of the orbitals, nine months of new treatments, and twelve additional rounds of chemotherapy, we'd been waiting for results from her spinal tap to reveal whether the latest approach had worked. This was why my father had called. My heart pounded so loudly in my chest, I thought I could hear it. I leaned my head against the wall behind me and looked up at the ceiling, phone to my ear. All my hopes, whispers, and dreams circled in my head. Memories of people laying hands on my mom and praying that God would heal her played like a movie reel in my mind. The truths I'd clung to in Scripture flashed like scenes before me. I gripped the phone tightly and steadied my shoulders, bracing myself for the weight of my father's words.

I don't remember the exact phrase he used, but I do remember I let out a guttural wail and fell to my knees and sobbed. As much as I believed I was prepared for the outcome, I hadn't known how it would feel.

Tears rolled down my face and I heard him say the doctors couldn't explain it. It was as if his voice was coming through a tunnel. My mother was a medical mystery. The cancer was now "undetectable," and although they wouldn't say she was cancer-free, they didn't know exactly how else to describe it. All the words that followed faded into a fog.

I was sobbing so hard my father had to stop talking to ask me if I was okay. Babbling like a lunatic, I uttered, "Yeah, I'm fine. I'm just so happy, and I feel like laughing, but all I can do is cry." In crying, I released the emotion of all the years spent wondering how God was going to answer. I knew what my mother believed, I knew what Scripture said, but persevering through this desert, through this fire, and seeing the promises of God miraculously manifested brought me inexplicable joy.

Nine years after I received that phone call from my father, I sat on a stool watching my mother bustle around like a busy bee as I got my hair done. She held a dress on a hanger in one hand and a pair of heels in the other. She hung up the dress and placed the shoes in the closet, stepping from side to side as if she were in the middle of a rhythmic dance. Her Puerto Rican heritage seeps out when she's busy; her hips sway to a beat only she can hear.

She was emotional but trying not to show it. A smile slipped across her face from time to time, and she gazed nostalgically out the hotel window. She seemed to be remembering a time long ago in a land far away.

She gently kissed my face as she passed by. Like a sage, she whispered wisdom to me, the kind of wisdom that is refined through trials, conceived in ecstasy and birthed in pain. As any good daughter does when she's blessed with a wise mother, I listened. My mother had earned that.

When we didn't have food in our refrigerator, my mother reminded us to pray for provisions. When we didn't have clothes, she recited Matthew 6:28 and promised that, just as the Lord dressed the lilies of the field, He would clothe us. When I didn't know if I would pass my college classes, she recalibrated my thinking and reminded me that God is the giver of all knowledge. She reminded me, in the words of James, that if we lack wisdom, we can ask for it, and God will provide liberally. And during my quarter-life crisis, my mother promised me that God had a plan and a purpose for my life.

Years later, she still poured out wisdom to her children. Whether it was how to fold fitted sheets or love our enemies, she always shared her best life secrets. Her words were a fountain, never a drain, and they overflowed into everyone she met.

She led her people into the wilderness, she survived her desert, she walked in the fire, and she lived to tell about all of it. Her wisdom was fashioned to endure and to withstand all the storms of life. Her very words were a testament to her loving, intimate relationship with the God she served.

Like Moses who spoke to God in the fire; like the children of Israel who were led by a pillar of fire; like Shadrach, Meshach, and Abednego who met God inside the fire; like the church of Acts that encountered God in the fire; like Job, refined like gold when he was tried by fire; like Jacqui Saburido, who survived being trapped in a fire; my mother arose from the ashes of affliction to boldly proclaim that her life had been made new. Her whispered wisdom was an invitation to trust in a God who invites us into the direst of circumstances, and who transforms us through the process.

As my mother bustled around my hotel room, I saw a woman who was in remission, a woman who was cancer-free. It was a pivotal day for both of us. On this day, I stared at a woman who had sung songs and cried out to God, who had wandered in the wilderness, who had begged God for transformation, and who was now flying free after rising from ashes, leading others to hear God speak and inherit the land promised to them.

THE PROMISE FULFILLED

The Israelite spies stood at the edge of their promise. They could see the journey ahead of them. They were chosen to inherit a land that was promised to them. And now twelve men—one from each tribe of Israel—were selected to check out the land and return with a report (Num. 13). These men had undoubtedly witnessed miracles. The parting of the Red Sea, manna falling from heaven, deliverance from slavery—they had witnessed firsthand the certainty of God's provision. But instead of feeling excitement that they would finally inherit the promise God had given to them, they were filled with terror, paralyzed by what was before them.

The spies came back from their reconnaissance mission with two things: fruit and fear. In their hands were symbols of the goodness of the land that was promised to them. But in their hearts was the impossibility of fortified walls, giants, and intimidating opponents. Waves of doubt covered God's children and clouded their memory of all the Lord had done for them since they left Egypt.

Although they were double-fisting—fruit in one hand and fear in the other—I couldn't begin to pass judgment here. I feel you, dear Israelites! Even now, after all I've seen, I hate to admit that I sometimes hold the fruit of the faithfulness of God while simultaneously gripping the fear He might not act again.

Only two of the twelve spies, Joshua and Caleb, believed they could take the land. They trusted it was theirs to inherit. They knew God was with them and had faith in His promises. And just maybe, although this is purely my own speculation, they didn't want to return to wandering in the desert. Ultimately, however, the other ten spies filled the Israelites with enough fear that they dissuaded the people from moving forward into the Promised Land. The Israelites' spirit of doubt was bigger than their trust in the deliverance they were promised. Their fear was bigger than their faith, and that decision cost them.

Because of their lack of faith forty years before, they were banished from the Promised Land and sentenced to years of wandering. But now the Israelites stood at the edge of their promise once again. After almost five hundred years of Egyptian captivity and over forty years of wandering in the desert, the children of God stood at the edge of freedom behind Moses' successor, Joshua. He stood on a precipice, in the same place he'd stood years before after the spies' initial exploratory expedition into the Promised Land. Joshua knew the truth—the Israelites had been released from captivity and slavery, but they had not received their promise. They had not received their whole freedom, not yet.

Faced with a decision, Joshua gave the order. Yes, the land was *still* full of giants. The land was *still* filled with the unknown. The land *still* contained impenetrable enemy walls. But the promise of God remained true. This time, the Israelites walked into that promise, as frightening as it may have seemed.

There is a difference between deliverance and freedom.

The Israelites were delivered from slavery, but stuck in the desert; they were not free. The Israelites had to learn that freedom takes courage, just like I did. To move out of our desert wilderness wanderings, we need to be willing to take a step into the unknown. There will come a time when we either believe God is who He says He is and can do what He says He can do, or we will continue to wander aimlessly because we are too afraid to inherit what has been promised to us.

THERE WILL COME A TIME WHEN WE EITHER BELIEVE GOD IS WHO HE SAYS HE IS AND CAN DO WHAT HE SAYS HE CAN DO, OR WE WILL CONTINUE TO WANDER AIMLESSLY BECAUSE WE ARE TOO AFRAID TO INHERIT WHAT HAS BEEN PROMISED TO US.

Joshua, the new leader, commissioned by Moses to take his place when he passed away (Deut. 31). Charged to lead his people into their destiny, Joshua relied on God's promise. Yes, the land was *still* full of giants. The land was *still* shrouded by the unknown. The land *still* contained impenetrable enemy walls. But the promise of God remained true. This time, the Israelites walked into that promise, as frightening as it must have seemed.

Joshua knew what the children of Israel would eventually realize: the God who promised the land would be faithful to fulfill that promise. The external circumstances hadn't changed, but the Israelites' internal posture had shifted, and finally, after forty years, they decided to trust the Lord.

When we stand at the edge of our promises, like the Israelites did, we must decide if we will move forward or stay in the desert. Will we push into the promises spoken by the fiery bush? Will we trust the same God who refines our faith, even in the crucible? *As God was faithful then, He is faithful now.*

Here's what I know—the issue at hand isn't God's ability to keep His word to us, but whether we'll trust Him enough to enter into our own Promised Lands in full faith.

WHAT A DIFFERENCE A BOOK MAKES

In the book of Numbers, God promised the Israelites the land they were to inherit (Num. 13:1). God literally said, "I'm giving them the land." It was a sealed deal. Done. Promised. Ensured. It wasn't about who they were, what they lacked, or the size of their people. It was about the faithfulness of their God. They had seen the miracles, but ignored the One who created the miracles.

In the book of Joshua, we see a new generation of Israelites who are standing at the edge of the Promised Land. They have to decide whether they are going to be fearful or faithful. Their decision will determine their destiny.

There will be desert seasons and wilderness wanderings and moments when we feel like we are in the fire. **But we must not lose perspective when we cannot see our future, because we know who holds the future.** The fulfillment of God's promises comes when we have the boldness to enter into the fire and embrace the transformation that takes place.

My mother—ever the student—used virtually every opportunity she found to teach us to move into the promise of God in the midst of the unknown. After the chemotherapy and the surgeries and the medications and finally, her remission, I was ecstatic! I wanted to shout from the mountaintops, holler from the valley, and scream at the top of my lungs that God had accomplished the impossible. He had fulfilled His promise! And now, she was with me as I entered into a new season, a new territory, a new land of promise. She danced around the room, reminding me of God's great faithfulness. She told me the God who freed the Israelites from slavery was the same God who provided for me in the wilderness. The One who'd led the children of Israel through the desert and into the Promised Land was leading me now. We serve a God who is with us in the beginning, middle, and end. We get to be—no, we *have* to be—strong and very courageous because that is what God requires when He is with us, just as He was with Joshua.

There in that room, dressed for my wedding, fully adorned in jewelry and with her hair coiffed to perfection, Mom moved like liquid. She was born to sway this way, I thought, from side to side, moving to an internal music that must have been more beautiful than the rest of us could imagine.

Later that night, with syncopated steps and joy-filled laughter, my mother danced the night away at my reception. Her newly highlighted short hair showed off her glowing skin. She wore a taupe dress with gold heels and jewelry that caught the light, reflecting sparkles on the surrounding walls. My dad laughed, cut in, and spun her around as I stood at the back watching them glide from one end of the dance floor to the other.

This was my Promised Land. Surrounded by my friends and family, I tasted the sweet fruit of my land of promise.

Virtual milk and honey flowed from goblets of change and chalices of endurance, and September 7, 2010 marked the end of one chapter in my story and the start of another.

Nine years of waiting, of desert thirst and blazing fire, ended completely in a single night. Stripped of all that I thought I wanted and left with only what I needed, I walked into a new fire, trusting God would continue to transform me into the person I was always meant to be.

That day it wasn't the vows I spoke, or the white gown I wore, or even the wonderful man I married that changed my life. *God* changed my life. I was finally living His promises.

These were my great discoveries on the road to the Promised Land: God wants to be *with* us, and He'll do whatever it takes. He'll let us wander into the deserts of our own making. He'll refine us in the furnace.

Maybe you're in your own desert. Maybe you feel lost and alone. Or maybe you are simply tired of crying out to God for help. And though you grow tired, my friend, push through and know that you are not alone in the fire. There is a God who hears you, and sees you, and loves you, and He is with you in the midst of the fire. Don't be afraid of the flames or the furnace, because it is in the midst of the fire that you will be changed. It is in the fire that you will experience the presence of God.

Let the journey start today, right now, in this moment. This is your invitation to play with fire.

Epilogue

The (Imperfect) Promised Land

So this is where fairy dust falls from the sky and we all live happily ever after, right? Nope, totally wrong. This isn't a Disney film, and I'm not a princess. (Unfortunately, because I would really like to wear a crown every day and have someone to make my bed every morning. But I digress.)

Just because we leave the desert doesn't mean we will live in a palace. Luxury and ease were never promised to the Israelites, even after they finally arrived in the Promised Land. Note that it was called the Promised Land, not the Perfect Land. In fact, God warned Joshua to be strong and courageous because He knew what peril Joshua and the Israelites would face. Thankfully, God was with them every step of the way.

As I entered new territory, joyful as it was, I don't think I was ready for a season of change. As beautiful as life was, there were still battles to fight—starting from within.

Everything I learned in my desert season was put to the test almost immediately.

I married a wonderful man who was previously married

and had two children. This family structure wasn't exactly the picturesque scenario I'd envisioned as a little girl. When I met Matt, however, I knew I wanted to spend the rest of my life with him. He is a strong man with great vision and is dedicated to building the church. (He is also a foot taller than me with sky blue eyes and broad shoulders. Rawr!) Hand to heaven, I knew eHarmony's compatibility algorithm actually worked because I wanted to figure out a way to make Matt fall in love with me by our second date. (Yes, we met on eHarmony, but that's another story for another day.)

We fell in love, and a year later, he proposed to me on a balcony overlooking the City of Angels.

But once we were married, I felt like my identity was altered right along with my new last name. I went from being a single, debt-free, indie-movie-watching, world-traveling woman to an instant stepmom of two, driving a sensible car, living in a small apartment in a new city on a budget. Everything changed, and it all happened at breakneck speed. (Remind me to tell you about the time I locked myself in my closet with a pillow and a bottle of water, swearing I was never leaving the closet. Fun times.) Although I wasn't exactly *prepared* for these sweeping changes, I welcomed step-parenting with open arms because I believed God knew what was perfect for me.

I left my job shortly after I got married and began working for A21, an anti-human trafficking organization. I was thrust into a terrible reality of the depravity of humankind. As I came face-to-face with survivors and heard the savage details of their treatment and abuse, I discovered a new battle to face, one ravaging nearly thirty million people across the globe. Work consumed my life, and I began struggling under the burden of millions of slaves crying out for freedom.

In the midst of this chaotic and new territory, I knew not to waver or wince or draw back. Like Jacqui Saburido, no matter what, I had to move forward. Even if *forward* meant doing things I didn't feel equipped to do.

Wisdom is surrounding yourself with people who have gone ahead and can remind you of your purpose. In a moment of vulnerability, I confessed to my boss that I felt overwhelmed and unfit to handle the new challenges in my life. She spoke a truth over me I will never forget: *God is preparing you for the thing He's prepared for you.* (Christine Caine is FULL of this wisdom.) I realized in that moment that everything I had gone through already had been preparation for what I was facing now. And this new season would prepare me for my next season. So we keep moving forward, holding on to the words spoken to Joshua: "Be strong and courageous."

Speaking of strong and courageous, Mom is still cancer-free and leading the church with my dad in the Los Angeles area. The oasis they dreamed of creating in the arid cityscape still remains, twenty-five years later. The only problem now is that the church is too small to hold all its congregants. They are believing for the funds to build a bigger home for weary desert travelers looking for refreshment. (It's time for Mom to make another prayer list! This time I will add: Move generous people to donate to an AWESOME church . . . so . . . if you know of rich people looking to invest, holler at your girl!)

I often look at Joshua's example as he led the Israelites into their Promised Land and spiritual inheritance. He rallied his people as they made their way and reminded them that he knew the land was theirs even forty years before they entered. With wisdom, confidence, and direction from God, he proclaimed, "I am still as strong today as the day Moses sent me out; I'm just as vigorous to go out to battle now as I was then" (Josh. 14:11). He fought valiantly and rose to lead the children of Israel into the land that was already theirs. We serve the same God today, and I believe *you* can find *your* Promised Land as well.

I may not have all the answers or a perfect life. I may not have mastered the ability to say no to fresh bread. But one thing I do know: I survived the fire and was refined by God to discover strength I never knew possible.

Everything that happens in your desert season—the crying out, the surrender, the belief in God's promises within community, and the patient listening to the Holy Spirit—is preparing you for your own Promised Land. You are able to do exceedingly abundantly more than you can think or imagine because our God is able to do exceedingly abundantly more than we can think or imagine.

Afterword

It was the day before Thanksgiving, and I received a FaceTime call from Bianca. What was supposed to be a holiday of gratitude and joy was met with lament and pain. Bianca called from a hotel room in a foreign country with tears streaming down her face and pain in her eyes. She choked back sobs as she told me she'd lost *all* of the final edits she'd worked on for her book. Weeks and weeks of hard work had simply vanished. Her manuscript was already four weeks late and with this setback, it looked like she might not make her publishing deadline.

Growing up, we had a family nickname for Bianca: *BB*. It stood for *Bocona Bianca,* which in Spanish means "Crybaby (loud mouth) Bianca." She cried easily and was very sensitive about wanting to do things right. Furthermore, when someone was harmed or wronged, she felt it empathetically. I stared at my adult daughter on my telephone screen, but saw the child she once was. BB was still sensitive, still caring, but I couldn't comfort her the way I used to.

As I did with all my five children growing up, I'd tuck Bianca into bed, gathering her into my arms in an attempt to demonstrate God's love and faithfulness to her by *being* loving and faithful. But as I stared into her tear-stained face decades later, I realized I couldn't father her the way our heavenly Father could. Bianca said she wanted this book to be a simple reminder of God's faithfulness, but in that moment, it felt like she had unintentionally forgotten it. She forgot about faithfulness. We prayed and believed this project would be completed and lives would be transformed through the simple message.

As any father might attest, you want your children to grow up and be the best version of themselves. You hope they achieve their potential and eventually help others do the same. But after reading this book, I saw my daughter beyond the tears of the missed deadline, beyond the dreams of writing words that matter. I saw my daughter as the woman who now tucks her children into bed, who gathers people around her dinner table, and who wraps strangers in her arms to show the love of God. Best yet, she's a woman who takes time to remember God's faithfulness.

Don't let the flames or dry lands scare you. As Bianca has been refined in the fire, I believe God can do the same for all us. Even in the moments when dreams (or edits) are lost, deadlines (book or otherwise) have been missed, or life is overwhelming, know that what will come of it will be greater than anything you lost. This I know to be true: as I raised her to love the Lord and believe in His faithfulness, she now is raising a generation to do the same. God has been faithful to me. God has been faithful to Bianca. And God will be faithful to you.

Pancho Juárez

Bianca's dad, Millie's husband, and father
to many at Calvary Chapel Montebello.

Acknowledgments

There are so many people to thank that I feel like a mosquito at a nudist colony: I don't know where to begin.

First and foremost, to the All-Consuming Fire: I'm crazy about You! Your promises move me to live in ways unthinkable. Thank You for transforming me into the bird who flies wildly, singing Your praises (albeit slightly off-key).

To the man who pushes me to be the best version of myself and who always believes I'm better than I am: Thank you, Matthew Ray. I'm wildly in love with you and know that God paired us together for a reason. For the nights you told me I could, for the days you told me I should, and for the weekends you reminded me I would, I'm forever grateful. I would've quit and run away from half the things I've accomplished if you weren't by my side. By your side I will always be until the day I breathe my last breath.

To Murmy and Papi: No hay suficientes palabras para decir lo mucho que te amo. Te debo todo. I owe you everything. Not only did you teach me how to read, you taught me how to learn. Thank you for always seeing me not for who I am, but for who I could be.

Mad love to BombSquad for the text messages, roll calls, prayers circles; to the Figs for being friends who stand with us when we fall down and pick us up when we can't stand; and to my dearest siblings, who walked me off of curbs that I thought were ledges. I'm a hot mess, but you all accept me for who I am. And for that simple fact, I will have your back forever and a day. Ryry and Parker: Thank you for dealing with me and all my crazy. I'm so proud to be your S'mom and I can't wait for all the memories we will make! Toni Trask, Mama Stella, and my CCM family (Loren, Rolo, Lisa, Eric, Juny, Derek, Carlitos, Abel, JP, Uncle Ivan, Denise, Monique, and every servant and member): You all were the best prayer partners, and I couldn't do half of what I do without your prayers and support. Special shout out to RJM for believing in me more than I believed in myself. To my work familia at A21 and Propel: We are changing the world, and there's no one else I'd want to work with.

A million thank yous go to Bryan Norman, Alive Literary, and Zondervan for allowing me to be part of their literary family, but special love goes to Carolyn McCready for allowing me to miss every deadline due to one random disaster after another in life, to Angela Scheff for being part of the beginning of this book, and to Tom Dean and Tim Schraeder for taking me on and making marketing magic. Sweet Harmony Harkema, you loved me well and spoke life over this project, for which I'm beyond grateful. Melanie Nyema Rozenblatt, there would be NO book without you. Hand to heaven, you are my LIFE editor and I love you. Special thanks to Seth Haines for jumping into deep waters with a crazy lady and helping put structure around my chaos. Your edits, words, and encouragement made this book what it is. To Suzanne "Zen" Physick, thank you for your patience, but more importantly, thank you for your love.

Lastly, to Christine Caine, Bob Goff, Don Miller, and Beth Moore, thank you for forcing me to not only write better stories but to LIVE a better story. I'm forever grateful for your mentorship (you may not know you have mentored me from afar) and valuing words more than platforms. Thank you for challenging me to play with fire.

(And if you read this page, too, thank you for staying through the whole journey. You're my favorite!)

For Further Reading

Who Is The Holy Spirit? R.C. Sproul, Reformation Trust Publishing, 2012

Forgotten God, Francis Chan, David C. Cook, 2009

Fresh Wind, Fresh Fire, Jim Cymbala, Zondervan, 1997

The Holy Spirit, Arthur W. Pink, multiple publishers, originally published 1932–1937

The Knowledge of the Holy, A.W. Tozer, HarperOne, originally published 1961

The Holy Spirit, Kevin DeYoung, Crossway Publications, 2011

The Person and Work of the Holy Spirit, R.A. Torrey, CreateSpace independent publishing, originally published 1910

Living Water: The Power of the Holy Spirit in Your Life, Chuck Smith, Word for Today, 2008

Living in the Power of the Holy Spirit, Charles Stanley, Thomas Nelson, 2005

Emotionally Healthy Spirituality, Peter Scazzero, Zondervan, 2006

Appendix: Spiritual Gifts

Scholars, theologians, and pastors have different views of spiritual gifts, what they entail, and even whether or not they still exist today. Some say only the gifts listed by Paul are acceptable; others argue not to limit God by the words of one man; and still others don't believe in the supernatural outworking of the Holy Spirit at all. I'm not here to argue one side or another, but I think it's important to know what gifts have been listed in the Bible. So here is a list of gifts listed in Scripture as an elementary guide (with biblical references for help). You're welcome!

Administration 1 Cor. 12:28

To steer the body toward the accomplishment of God-given goals and directives by planning, organizing, and supervising others (Greek Word: kubernesis-to steer, guide, helmsmen).

Apostle Eph. 4:11; 1 Cor. 12:28

To be sent forth to new frontiers with the gospel, providing leadership over church bodies and maintaining authority over spiritual matters pertaining to the church (Greek Word: apostolos-'apo'=from 'stello'=send; one sent forth).

Celibacy 1 Cor. 7:7, 8

To voluntarily remain single without regret and with the ability to maintain controlled sexual impulses so as to serve the Lord without distraction.

Discernment 1 Cor. 12:10

To clearly distinguish truth from error by judging whether the behavior or teaching is from God, Satan, human error, or human power.

Evangelism Eph. 4:11

To be a messenger of the good news of the Gospel (Greek Word: euaggelistes-preacher of gospel; eu=well, angelos=message-messenger of good).

Exhortation Rom. 12:8

To come alongside of someone with words of encouragement, comfort, consolation, and counsel to help them be all God wants them to be (Greek Word: paraklesis-calling to one's side)

Faith 1 Cor. 12:8–10

To be firmly persuaded of God's power and promises to accomplish His will and purpose and to display such a confidence in Him and His Word that circumstances and obstacles do not shake that conviction.

Giving Rom. 12:8

To share what material resources you have with liberality and cheerfulness without thought of return.

Healing 1 Cor. 12:9, 28, 30

To be used as a means through which God makes people whole (either physically, emotionally, mentally, or spiritually).

Helps 1 Cor. 12:28

To offer support or assistance to others in the body so as to free them up for ministry.

Hospitality 1 Peter 4:9, 10

To warmly welcome people, even strangers, into one's home or church as a means of serving those in need of food or lodging (Greek Word: philoxenos-love of strangers; 'philos'=love; 'xenos'=stranger).

Knowledge 1 Cor. 12:8

To seek to learn as much about the Bible as possible through the gathering of much information and the analyzing of that data

Leadership Rom. 12:8

To stand before the people in such a way as to attend to the direction of the body with such care and diligence so as to motivate others to get involved in the accomplishment of these goals.

Martyrdom 1 Cor. 13:3

To give over one's life to suffer or to be put to death for the cause of Christ.

Mercy Rom. 12:8

To be sensitive toward those who are suffering, whether physically, mentally, or emotionally, so as to feel genuine sympathy with their misery, speaking words of compassion but moreso caring for them with deeds of love to help alleviate their distress.

Miracles 1 Cor. 12:10, 28

To be enabled by God to perform mighty deeds which witnesses acknowledge to be of supernatural origin and means.

Missionary Eph. 3:6–8

To be able to minister in another culture.

Pastor Eph. 4:11

To be responsible for spiritually caring for, protecting, guiding, and feeding a group of believers entrusted to one's care

Prophecy Rom. 12:6; 1 Cor. 12:10; Eph. 4:11

To speak forth the message of God to His people (Greek Word: prophetes-the forth-telling of the will of God; 'pro'=forth; 'phemi'=to speak)

Service Rom. 12:7

To identify undone tasks in God's work, however menial, and use available resources to get the job done (Greek Word: diakonia-deacon, attendant 'diako'=to run errands).

Teaching Rom. 12:7; 1 Cor. 12:28; Eph. 4:11

To instruct others in the Bible in a logical, systematic way so as to communicate pertinent information for true understanding and growth

Tongues 1 Cor. 12:10; 14:27–28

To speak in a language not previously learned so unbelievers can hear God's message in their own language or the body be edified.

Interpretation of Tongues 1 Cor. 12:10; 14:27, 28

To translate the message of someone who has spoken in tongues.

Voluntary Poverty 1 Cor. 13:3

To purposely live an impoverished lifestyle to serve and aid others with your material resources.

Wisdom 1 Cor. 12:8

To apply knowledge to life in such a way as to make spiritual truths quite relevant and practical in proper decision-making and daily life situations.